MEAL PREP *in an*

INSTANT

56 LIGHTENED-UP RECIPES AND 7 PREP PLANS FOR YOUR INSTANT POT®

MEAL PREP *in an* INSTANT

56 LIGHTENED-UP RECIPES AND 7 PREP PLANS FOR YOUR INSTANT POT®

Use of the trademarks is authorized by Instant Brands Inc., owner of Instant Pot®

BECCA LUDLUM

ALPHA

Publisher Mike Sanders
Editor Brook Farling
Designer Lindsay Dobbs
Art Director William Thomas
Photographer Kelley Jordan Schuyler
Food Stylist Lovoni Walker
Chef Ashley Brooks
Recipe Tester Kat Hodson
Proofreaders Lisa Starnes and Rick Kughen
Indexer Celia McCoy

First American Edition, 2020
Published in the United States by DK Publishing
6081 E. 82nd Street, Indianapolis, Indiana 46250

19 20 21 22 23 10 9 8 7 6 5 4 3 2 1
001–317438–DEC2020

ISBN 978-1-4654-9341-5
Library of Congress Catalog Number: 2020931144

DK books are available at special discounts when purchased in
bulk for sales promotions, premiums, fund-raising,
or educational use. For details, contact:
DK Publishing Special Markets,
1450 Broadway, Suite 801, New York, NY 10018
SpecialSales@dk.com

Author photo © Becca Ludlum
All other images © Dorling Kindersley Limited
For further information see: www.dkimages.com

Printed and bound in China

For the curious
www.dk.com

ABOUT THE AUTHOR

Becca Ludlum is a nutrition coach and lifestyle blogger at mycrazygoodlife.com, where she helps readers learn more about the food they eat, while sharing the delicious recipes she is making for her family. She is an advocate for eating whole foods and believes the foods we choose to eat can impact our overall health, weight, and lifestyle. While she focuses on eating the best that she can the majority of the time, she understands that balance is everything and has never turned down a homemade brownie.

Becca lives in Tucson, Arizona, and loves to develop, test, and photograph recipes that satisfy and feel indulgent, while still using minimally processed ingredients. When Becca isn't spending time with her family and friends, practicing at her local yoga studio, or attending hip-hop concerts, you'll find her in the kitchen testing new recipes and refining them to be as simple and tasty as possible.

ACKNOWLEDGMENTS

Writing a book is not a one-woman show, and this would not have been possible without an army of support from my family and friends.

I'd like to start by saying thank you to Steve for keeping me on track with deadlines, providing pep talks throughout the writing process, and being my rock in every situation, like when I forget to move my Instant Pot valve and panic because my pot isn't sealing.

Michael and Jack, thank you for sharing your polite but honest feedback for every recipe in this book. I love you for happily eating the same meals over and over (and over) without complaint—I could not have perfected these recipes without your suggestions. You're both my favorite.

Rachael, I smile looking back at all the brainstorming, testing, and troubleshooting you've done with me on these recipes. I treasure your friendship, and I am grateful for you—especially when you send me motivating hip-hop lyrics. Thank you.

Mom and Dad, thank you for supporting me in writing this book—and also in every single thing I've ever done…ever.

Thank you to Wayne, Ty, and Solána for inspiring my creativity and keeping me company in the kitchen day and night.

Brook, thank you for teaching me how to write a book. I've learned so very much during this process, and am grateful for your kindness and knowledge.

To every one of my friends who tested and tasted recipes, shared feedback, and offered cocktails at the end of the longest days—thank you.

CONTENTS

INTRODUCTION

Trying to fit everything into each 24-hour day is kind of like working a jigsaw puzzle that has too many pieces. Work, exercise, house chores, family time, friend time, me time, food, and health—it can all get overwhelming very quickly.

Food is fuel for your body, but I believe it should also be delicious and enjoyable. Food is something that nourishes us and brings family and friends together around a table, helping us create memories and traditions. This book is full of healthy recipes that were created using minimally processed ingredients and a balance of whole grains, healthy fats, and lots of vegetables. Also, healthy doesn't mean skipping dessert! Rest assured that the desserts in this book are made with whole grains and contain no refined sugars.

Creating delicious recipes is something I've been doing online for several years at MyCrazyGoodLife.com. My community has grown into millions of readers who love the simple ingredients and satisfying recipes I share. The meals in this book are straight from my kitchen, and they've been tested time and time again by my family and friends. These are our favorites—the ones that made my kids say, "Mom, this has to go in the book."

Meal prep is how I make the puzzle pieces fit together perfectly—it's the foundation of a productive kitchen. Meal prep allows me to set aside time one day a week to cook so I can be extra productive on the other six. Adding the Instant Pot to the mix gives me a way to multitask like a champ because, for most recipes, I can simply add ingredients to the pot and walk away to clean dishes, cut vegetables, or get ready for the next recipe while the Instant Pot cooks.

Throughout this book, I've utilized a variety of cooking methods to help you become familiar with Instant Pot cooking. I used a 6-quart Instant Pot DUO to test all of the recipes in this book and used multiple Instant Pot functions, cooked both frozen and thawed ingredients, and made many of the meals and sides right in the pot together.

I hope this book helps you learn how to meal prep and cook delicious food in your Instant Pot, all while allowing you to carve out more time in your life for the important things like exercise, your favorite hobbies, and lots of laughs with family and friends.

Becca Ludlum

MEAL PREP ESSENTIALS

WELCOME TO MEAL PREP WITH THE INSTANT POT!

There are a variety of reasons why people choose to meal prep with an Instant Pot: to save time, save money, and eat healthier. However, the thought of preparing an entire week's worth of breakfasts, lunches, and dinners can be overwhelming for some, so I want to answer some common questions, and explain why it's worth it and why you'll learn to love it!

Why should you meal prep?

Meal prep can save you time by allowing you to focus on preparing and cooking several recipes simultaneously and doing so in just a few hours one day a week. By following a prep plan, you'll be preparing ingredients for one recipe while another recipe cooks in the Instant Pot. You'll also be shopping for multiple recipes at once and utilizing ingredients across multiple recipes. The end result will be a week's worth of meals that are ready to be pulled out of the fridge or freezer and simply reheated. Instead of you having to come home and cook a different meal every evening or prepare a new lunch every day, all you'll need to do is reheat!

Meal prep is a great way to save money because you'll be following the grocery lists that are included with each plan. Now you won't have to make those last-minute trips to the grocery store during the week that can result in you buying groceries for one meal at a time, which can be expensive. Instead, you'll be following a detailed prep plan that will allow you to purchase everything you need in one trip, while maximizing the ingredients you have available and minimizing food waste. You'll also eat healthier because you'll be planning and preparing healthy meals in advance, which means you'll be less likely to reach for junk food or eat fast food.

What's the difference between meal planning and meal prep?

Meal planning and meal prep often are confused with one another, but they both are important steps in the meal prep process. Meal planning is simply the process of creating a plan for the meals you'll be cooking and eating for a week, and then making a detailed grocery list to shop for those meals. Meal prep is the process of following a detailed, one-day prep plan to prep and cook all or some of the weekly meals in advance instead of cooking different meals each night. Prepped meals can then be refrigerated or frozen and simply reheated when you're ready to eat. With meal prep, you do the prep and cooking on a single day of the week, but you'll enjoy healthy meals throughout the week.

How long does it take to complete a prep session?

It typically takes me 3–5 hours to prep my meals for the week, depending on what recipes I'm making. If I use my time efficiently, however, I'm able to finish most plans in around 3–3½ hours. When prepping, I try to stay laser focused on the task at hand and don't allow my attention to become diverted—it's the secret for getting my prep done on time.

How does the Instant Pot make meal prep better?

The Instant Pot is your secret meal prep weapon! The Instant Pot is an amazing appliance that allows you to pressure cook, sauté, slow cook, and more. It means you won't need to utilize lots of different appliances or dirty up stacks of pots and pans for your prep because most of your meals are made right in the pot. And because the Instant Pot cooks to very precise temperatures and times, you aren't left to worry about overcooking a dish on the stovetop or in the oven; while the Instant Pot works its magic, you can spend your time preparing ingredients for the next recipe.

Can I create my own plans?

If you choose to create your own prep plans, it's important to create a detailed shopping list and prep plan so you can manage your time efficiently. If you decide to make five recipes on a prep day but don't have a plan to utilize your time efficiently, a prep day could easily take you 6–8 hours to complete. This is why it's important to make meals specifically designed for prepping. I consider meals perfect for prepping if they're hearty, easy to prepare, will last in the fridge for several days, and can be easily frozen and reheated.

Can I use my own recipes in a prep plan?

If you choose to create a plan from your own recipes, you should choose recipes that are hearty, and also freeze and reheat well. Chicken and rice dishes, pasta dishes, and oatmeal recipes are all ideal for meal prep because they can be made in large batches and then refrigerated or frozen. Most of the recipes in this book fall into this category and include instructions for freezing and reheating. However, some recipes do contain fresh ingredients that can break down in storage after a day or two, so those recipes are best made fresh and in two batches.

GETTING STARTED

If you're new to meal prep, it might feel a bit overwhelming at first, but once you have a plan or two under your belt, it will quickly become a routine that you'll look forward to every week! Sometimes new preppers discover it's better to start with a simpler plan, so I've created some guidelines to help you find your footing and get you started.

DETERMINE WHAT LEVEL OF PREP IS RIGHT FOR YOU

Every household has different meal prep needs, and in order to be successful, you'll first want to determine which level is best for you. I've categorized meal prep into three levels to help you find one that works best. There is no one-size-fits-all for meal prepping, so start slowly and experiment to find the approach that works best for you.

LUNCHES ONLY

Some new preppers prefer to dive into meal prep by first preparing only lunches. This approach is useful if you prefer to cook dinner every night and make breakfast every morning, but you find you still like the convenience of having your lunches for the week prepped and ready to go. Lots of busy professionals find this is a great way to get started with meal prep.

BREAKFASTS AND LUNCHES

I love the routine of making dinner every night, so quite often this is how we prep in my house. If I know it'll be a busy week, I'll only prep the ingredients for dinners and then cook dinner each night.

BREAKFASTS, LUNCHES, & DINNERS

This level is for the person who wants it all planned out for the week—every meal is ready to go on Monday morning. The plans in this book are written with this approach in mind and will help you prepare a full week's worth of delicious meals that you can pull straight from the fridge or freezer and simply reheat.

Using the Recipes

 gluten-free  dairy-free

Every recipe in this book includes estimated prep and pressure times as well as total recipe times that account for other factors like pressure build and pressure release. The recipe's times are estimated and can be impacted by a number of factors, so variations in total cook times

should be expected. Also, you'll notice that most recipes include icons that indicate if a recipe is gluten-free or dairy-free. Also included with several recipes are tips that give instructions for how to make a recipe dairy-free or gluten-free, or how to add different flavor profiles.

CHOOSE YOUR PREP METHOD

There is no one-size-fits-all approach to meal prep, so it's important that you find the method that works best for you. And don't feel like you can't change your approach if the method that is utilized in this book doesn't work for you—you might find that a combination of methods is what works best. Here are some of the most common forms of meal prep methods that preppers tend to follow.

PREP, COOK, AND THEN REFRIGERATE OR FREEZE METHOD

There are many different ways to meal prep, but this book is written using the prep, cook, then refrigerate or freeze method. This method is, by far, the most popular with preppers. With this method, I love that I can cook everything and then place meals for the next several days in the fridge or freezer. Because reheating meals is something that I don't mind doing, this type of prep works best for my family. If you're prepping for one person, this type of prep is perfect because you can refrigerate or freeze your meals in single servings and then reheat them later without worrying if food is going to go to waste.

PREP, FREEZE, AND THEN COOK METHOD

Some preppers prefer a prep, freeze, then cook approach. This method is good for those who prefer not to eat leftover-style meals or prefer not to have their fridges or freezers full of meal prep containers. If you like to cook every day but like to have all of the prep work done in advance, this type of prep is perfect for you; just make sure you have ample freezer space for the prepped meals and a bit of knowledge about cooking recipes from frozen in the Instant Pot. Here's a helpful tip if you're following this method: Freeze your prepped, uncooked meals in round containers, so when it's time to cook lunch or dinner, you can partially defrost them in the fridge and then simply stick them right in the Instant Pot.

INGREDIENTS-ONLY PREP METHOD

If preferred, you can perform an ingredients-only prep where you'll wash and cut all of the ingredients that you'll be cooking later in the week. When I perform an ingredients-only prep, I like to clean and dry all fruits and vegetables and then cut the ones I know will hold up in the fridge. I also like to preportion any meats that I'll need and place them in the fridge or freezer along with any seasonings or marinades that I'll be using in the recipes.

It's worth mentioning that not all uncooked ingredients are hearty enough to sit in the fridge all week, so an ingredients-only prep is best done only with certain ingredients. Some meats or vegetables won't hold up as well if they're cut and left to sit in the fridge for a couple of days. This, in combination with some people's preferences to not cook certain ingredients like eggs ahead of time, means that you should consider whether the ingredients for a recipe will hold up in the fridge for five days before including it in your weekly prep.

You might find that it could take a few weeks of trial and error to find the correct combination of meal prep methods that works best for you and your family, and that's okay. Don't feel that meal prep is an all or nothing concept—it's an evolution. You'll get better at it as the weeks go by and you get a few prep sessions underneath your belt.

TIPS FOR MEAL PREP SUCCESS

I've had a lot of experience with meal prep, and I can tell you the Instant Pot changes the meal prep game! It allows you to start a recipe and then walk away from the pot while the meal is cooking, allowing you to spend more time prepping other recipes.

USING THE PREP PLANS IN THIS BOOK

The prep plans in this book are intended to feed a small family for five days with three lunch or dinner recipes and one breakfast recipe. However, because most of the recipes in this book follow a prep, cook, and then refrigerate or freeze approach, anyone can use this book, even if you're cooking for just one or two. Each prep plan includes four primary recipes, but also included with each plan are four alternate recipes that can be exchanged in case a particular recipe in a plan doesn't suit your tastes.

Each plan also includes a detailed shopping list that tells you exactly what you'll need to purchase to create the four primary recipes, as well as a basic equipment list that will help you plan your prep day more efficiently. The prep plans include estimated times and are written in a way that is intended to help you maximize your time in the kitchen, but be patient and don't get frustrated if the plans take longer than expected. These plans will yield a lot of meals that

can be enjoyed for days or even weeks, so if you prefer to break the plan up over a few days, or just make a few of the recipes, that's okay.

The Freezer is Your Friend

We've all had plans that have changed because something unexpected comes up. If I've prepped meals for the week and my plans change, it's important to me to not waste the food I've made, so I immediately move some or all of my prepped meals to the freezer. There is no harm in freezing a meal to thaw and reheat later, but leaving uneaten meals in the refrigerator for longer than necessary can result in them going bad, which means they end up being discarded.

If you find that you've ended up with more food than you can eat in a week, freeze some servings and reserve a few in the fridge. Most recipes in this book can be frozen for weeks or even months. (I'll often add previously prepped and frozen meals to another week's plan to provide some variety and also make my next prep week easier.) If you store your meals in freezer-safe containers and label them with the recipe names and made-on dates, you'll find you won't be wasting food.

MAKING THE MOST OF YOUR PREP DAY

Here are some simple tips for success when planning your own meal prep day.

- **Cook and freeze extra staples during your prep days.** Increase the amount of veggies or grains that you cook and freeze during each prep session, especially if you know you're going to be busy the following week. Those extras often are used across multiple recipes and can be thawed and reheated.

- **Don't fret if you make too much (or too little).** If you get to the middle of the week and have more food than you envisioned eating, freeze some in single servings. This will allow you to mix up your meals for the next week by defrosting and heating up one of those frozen meals. If you find yourself running out of food midweek, spend an hour during the week prepping an easier recipe that will last you through the weekend. When this happens to me, I like utilizing the vegetables I have on hand to make a single batch of a hearty recipe like Loaded Vegetable Goulash since it's quick to prep, easy to cook, and freezes well.

- **Use your time efficiently.** Meal prep can easily last all day if you're not organized. Try to be as efficient as possible and never stop moving during a prep session. While one recipe is cooking in the pot, you should start prepping the next recipe. As soon as a recipe is finished cooking, promptly separate it into containers and move on to the next recipe.

- **Stay flexible.** You don't need to prep every meal in a prep plan to completion for the prep session to be successful. Some recipes are best made to completion and transferred to the fridge and freezer promptly, but if you find that breaking up a prep session across multiple days works better for you, then go for it!

- **Customize the plans to work for you.** If you prefer cooking dinner every night, you can just prep your breakfasts and lunches. I've found that people who have an all-or-nothing mindset about meal prep tend to give up on it, so focus on finding the prep level that works best for you and your family.

CREATING YOUR OWN PREP PLAN

If you want to customize the prep plans included in this book and substitute alternate recipes, following these steps will help you help maximize your time.

1. **Choose your recipes.** The prep plans in this book feature three primary lunch and dinner recipes and one breakfast recipe, but you can mix and match the recipes to suit your family's needs and tastes. As a general rule, I don't recommend prepping more than four recipes in a session unless you're okay with spending a good portion of your prep day in the kitchen. In addition to the meals, I also like to create a list of snacks to prep in case I have a few extra minutes of time while things are cooking.

2. **Assemble your shopping list and source your ingredients.** Each prep plan in this book includes a complete shopping list to help make sourcing ingredients easier. However, if you're building your own prep plan, you'll need to create your own shopping list to source the ingredients for the recipes you've selected. I find it helps to break your shopping list into the same categories used in the shopping lists for the prep plans in this book. This will help you better determine what you already have on hand, what you still need to buy, and how many recipes will use the same ingredients (so you don't overbuy).

3. **Write out your prep plan.** Begin making your plan by determining which recipe requires the least amount of prepping, and then plan to make that recipe first. Determine which recipes will require longer cook times in the pot and which recipes have shorter times in the pot, then plan your ingredients prep to fill those gaps where the pot will be in use. The key is to utilize your time as efficiently as possible during your prep session and always be prepping ingredients and cleaning up when you have time to do so.

4. **Assemble your equipment list.** Read through the recipes and make a quick list of what equipment you'll need to prepare all of the recipes. It will help you utilize the same equipment for multiple recipes, and it will also help reduce the amount of cleanup.

ESSENTIAL INSTANT POT ACCESSORIES

Although I've purchased many Instant Pot accessories, I find myself really only needing a few. These accessories help me make more food in the pot, allow me to create fun recipes that I wouldn't normally make, and also allow me to step away from the Instant Pot even more than normal. (I love not being tied to the kitchen while I'm making dinner!) These accessories are used in several recipes in this book and are essential to have on hand.

TRIVET
Included with all Instant Pot models

The metal trivet that comes with your Instant Pot is used to keep certain foods off the bottom of the pot and is your most essential accessory. Because all recipes need liquid for the pot to come to pressure, anything cooked directly in the Instant Pot will be submerged in liquid unless it's resting on the trivet. While it's okay to cook some foods directly in liquid, there are others that need to be kept away from the liquid and the heating element at the bottom of the pot, which can burn some foods.

There are other benefits of using the trivet. Using it under a cake pan or oven-safe dish will promote more even cooking, and using it when steaming vegetables or cooking potatoes will help keep them from getting soggy. The trivet can also help you remove large pieces of meat and other accessories—like silicone molds—more easily from the pot.

The trivet is also helpful for keeping certain foods separated in the pot. In a recipe like the Teriyaki Meatball Bowls (p. 60), you'll be adding the rice and liquid to the bottom of the pot, then placing the trivet and egg bite molds on top. This helps keep the foods separated, but still allows them to be cooked together.

SEALING RINGS
Available for 3-, 6-, and 8-quart Instant Pot models

Your Instant Pot sealing ring is a workhorse—it's what creates the airtight seal that allows your pot to come to pressure. However, because it's inside the pot for every cooking cycle, it tends to deteriorate a bit every time you use it, and it absorbs a lot of cooking odors—particularly the first time you use it.

And when a sealing ring stops sealing, it doesn't do so slowly over time—it's a sudden event, and it has happened to me on more than one occasion. Because of this, I like to keep a few backup rings on hand in case one stops working. I also like to keep different colored rings on hand for cooking different types of foods. I like to use a red ring for aromatic foods like chili, meatloaf, or stir-frys, while I use a blue ring for less aromatic foods like rice, desserts, and eggs. This little trick helps ensure that my desserts will never absorb the smell of last night's chili and also ensures that I'll always have a backup on hand in case one fails.

I recommend cleaning your sealing rings after every 5 to 6 cooking cycles in the pot. You can wash them by hand in hot, soapy water, or they can be washed in the dishwasher.

INSTANT POT ROUND CAKE PAN
Size: 7 inches (diameter) by 3 inches (height); available for 6- and 8-quart Instant Pot models

If a recipe in this book calls for a baking pan or oven-safe dish, this is the one I used to test the recipe. It's reasonably priced, very thin (so it doesn't add a lot of cooking time to your recipes), holds a high volume of food, and will help reduce the chances of overcooking your food and thus receiving those annoying burn warnings. Do note that when cooking with this pan, you must cover it with a silicone cover or aluminum foil to help keep other liquids from getting into the pan while the food is cooking.

If you don't have this accessory, you also can use an oven-safe dish that measures no more than 7 inches in diameter by 3 inches in depth, but be aware that some thicker casserole dishes might add extra cook time to your recipes, and they also might not have the capacity to hold all of the ingredients without exceeding the maximum fill line.

EGG BITE MOLDS
Size: 8.25 inches (diameter) by 2 inches (height); available for 3-, 6-, and 8-quart Instant Pot models

These silicone molds have so many uses—you can use them to make small desserts, snacks, meatballs, and even cupcakes! However, because only two molds fit in the Instant Pot at once, you'll be limited to 14 servings of whatever you're cooking. (I've found that's more than plenty for most recipes.) You can also use these to freeze extra ingredients in small portions; each cup holds about ⅓ cup of broth, sauce, or other "extras" that you don't want to go to waste. Note that because they are open at the top, egg bite molds have to be covered with aluminum foil or a silicone cover while being used in the Instant Pot. Most molds will come with lids for storage, but these lids are not safe for use in the Instant Pot.

If you don't have an egg bite mold, you can use ramekins, silicone cupcake liners, or oven-safe glass jars for making smaller batches.

COOKING WITH THE INSTANT POT

Learning how to cook with an Instant Pot can be a bit intimidating at first, but with a little practice and experience, you'll quickly realize how amazing this little appliance really is. I've been cooking with an Instant Pot for several years now, and have pulled together some helpful information to help you get the most out of your Instant Pot.

USING LIQUIDS IN THE INSTANT POT

All pressure cookers need liquid to come to pressure and cook food. Most recipes use water and broth or stock, but some recipes also use the cooking liquids from frozen meats or liquids from ingredients like canned peppers or diced tomatoes. The amount of liquid your pot will require to come to pressure will vary depending on the size of your Instant Pot, so always stick to the recommendations in the recipes or in your user manual to ensure recipes turn out how you're expecting.

FINISHING FOODS THAT AREN'T FULLY COOKED

If a recipe doesn't appear to be fully cooked, you can close the lid and set the cook time again. If it's apparent that a recipe needs additional cooking time, close the lid and set the pressure time for an additional 5–7 minutes; the pot will come to pressure more quickly the second time around and will continue to cook the food as the pot comes to pressure. If the food just needs another couple of minutes of cooking, set the cook time to zero (0) minutes; it will come to pressure and then immediately begin to release the pressure. If the food appears to be fully cooked, but you just prefer it be a little more done, simply close the lid and don't set the cook time; the remaining heat in the pot will continue to cook the food.

ADJUSTING COOKING TIMES WHEN DOUBLING RECIPES

Typically, a doubled recipe doesn't require twice the cooking time because a pressure cooker cooks based on the thickness or size of the ingredients and not necessarily the quantity. For example, one small chicken breast will cook in the same amount of time as four small chicken breasts, but larger chicken breasts will need additional cooking time. Also, when doubling a recipe, it's important to ensure that the recipe fits into the pot and sits below the maximum fill line mark in the inner pot. Doubling the amounts of pasta, rice, or beans in a recipe does not require increases in cook times, but these foods will expand while cooking, so make sure any doubled recipes that contain these foods are safely below the maximum fill line. These foods also absorb liquids as they cook, so be sure to maintain a consistent food-to-liquid ratio when doubling ingredients.

USING THAWED INGREDIENTS VERSUS FROZEN INGREDIENTS

Always try to use exactly what is specified in the recipe. If a recipe calls for thawed meat, using frozen meat could mean the pot will take longer to come to pressure, which could result in other ingredients being overcooked. Conversely, if a recipe calls for frozen meat, using thawed meat could result in the meat being overcooked.

MAKING A FOIL SLING TO PREVENT BURNS

If you're using an oven-safe dish to cook a recipe, it's important to be able to get the dish out of the pot without burning your hands. If you don't have a trivet or if it's too difficult to grasp the trivet handles and safely remove the dish from the pot, you can make a foil sling to place under the dish. To do so, cut a large piece of foil about 24 inches long, fold it lengthwise into thirds, and then place the dish in the middle of the sling. Grasp the ends of the sling to carefully lower the dish into the pot. When the cook time is complete, grasp the ends of the sling to carefully lift the dish out of the pot.

USING POT-IN-POT (PIP) COOKING

Pot-in-pot cooking (or PIP, as many Instant Pot enthusiasts like to call it) involves cooking in a secondary dish that is placed inside the inner pot. There are a few reasons to do this. It allows for more even cooking because the heating element isn't directly underneath the food, and it reduces the chances of receiving a burn warning because the dish is elevated above the bottom of the pot. It also makes it easier to serve food straight from a dish rather than trying to serve it directly from the Instant Pot or transferring it from the pot to a serving dish. It's important to note that the type and size of dish you use can affect your results. If the dish is too small to hold a recipe, you may need to divide it in half and cook it in two batches.

Why do cook and build times tend to vary in the Instant Pot?

The Instant Pot is an incredibly versatile and dependable appliance; however, that doesn't mean that everyone gets the same results every time they use it. A lot of variables can affect how long it can take for your pot to come to pressure and how long it can take for food to cook. Differences in elevation, how much food is in the pot, and the temperature of the food when it goes into the pot can all cause the cook and pressure times to vary—even a leaky sealing ring can have an effect.

If your recipes aren't cooking the way you expect them to or if the pot is taking considerably longer to come to pressure than you're expecting, try replacing the sealing ring or adjusting the cooking times for differences in elevation. To adjust for differences in elevation, add an additional 5% cooking time for every 1,000 feet above 2,000 feet in elevation. If you are below 2,000 feet in elevation, reduce the cooking time by 5% for every 1,000 feet in elevation below 2,000 feet. Also, if you find that your pot consistently seems to take longer to come to pressure than it should, try pressing **Sauté** and cooking the food for a few minutes before sealing the pot and selecting the pressure setting. This will help heat the food and bring the pot to pressure more quickly.

STORING INGREDIENTS

One thing all meal preppers struggle with is how to keep uncooked ingredients fresh in the refrigerator before they are ready to be prepped and cooked. Here are some helpful tips for keeping your ingredients as fresh as possible before you begin your prep session.

STORING FRESH PRODUCE

The first thing I do when I get home from the grocery store is gently wash and dry all produce, except for items with thick, inedible skins like onions, pineapples, and avocados. I then allow the produce to dry on a clean drying mat for at least one hour before storing. Damp produce won't last as long in the fridge, so it's always best to let it air dry really well. I like to do this for fresh herbs as well—especially cilantro and parsley. A salad spinner can help with drying herbs, or you can wrap them in paper towels and tap the wrap on the countertop several times to shake the moisture loose. Any dampness on herbs will reduce their lifespans, so make sure fresh herbs are dry before being stored in the fridge.

Produce items with high water contents like cucumbers or bell peppers are best cut the day you use them. Snacking vegetables like carrots and celery will keep well in the fridge for a few days, so I often use down time on prep days to peel and slice these items into snack-sized pieces. If you need them to last longer, there are produce containers that have a grate at the bottom that keeps the vegetables from sitting directly in condensation from the fridge, which can make them spoil more quickly.

You can also store produce in mesh produce bags. If you don't have mesh produce bags, you can store fresh items in the plastic produce bags from the grocery store, just so long as the bags and produce are both dry before you refrigerate them.

Finally, don't overcrowd the produce drawers in your refrigerator. Overcrowding can keep air flow from reaching your produce, which can allow mold to build up and promote spoilage. I try to create "pockets" of produce in my refrigerator with gaps in between to avoid overcrowding.

STORING FRESH MEAT

It might seem a bit strange to come home from the grocery store and immediately put chicken in the freezer, particularly if you know you'll be cooking it the next day, but there's good reason to do so. A recipe will have a longer cook time with frozen meat, and sometimes that longer cook time is needed to cook other items in the pot. Using frozen meats in a recipe means the Instant Pot will take longer to come to pressure. Even as the pot is coming to pressure, it's cooking the ingredients, and it will continue to cook even after the pressure time has ended and pressure is being released from the pot, so ensuring the meat goes into the pot exactly as it's written in the recipe is important.

It's fairly easy to store both refrigerated and frozen meats for later use. I often remove meat from the store package when I get home from shopping and place it in a thick freezer bag if I need to freeze it. If the meat is purchased in large chunks, such as the case might be with something like flank steak, I will cut it into smaller slices before freezing it. Fresh meat should be stored in the refrigerator for no more than 3 days.

If you're not planning on using meat within that time frame, you should transfer it to the freezer so it doesn't spoil.

It's also helpful to season meats before storing if you know how you'll be using them later. I often buy chicken breasts and add the marinade to the bag before freezing so I can simply remove them from the freezer, thaw, and go straight to cooking.

USING YOUR FREEZER FOR STORING PREPPED INGREDIENTS

If you have time to make some extra staples and freeze them, I highly recommend doing this as a way to cut down on the length of your prep days. Every week, I like to cook extra rice, quinoa, and vegetables and use my freezer to store what I've made for future meal prep recipes.

Making extra rice, quinoa, and vegetables takes approximately the same amount of time in the Instant Pot, whether you're cooking smaller or larger volumes. You can easily freeze leftover staples for use in weekday meals or for use on a future prep day. I also love being able to grab these items out of the freezer on weeks that we don't meal prep and add them to quick meals. It's important to note that while most grains freeze well and can be frozen for several months, some cooked vegetables may not freeze as well.

HEALTHY INGREDIENTS & SWAPS

In order to get the most out of the Instant Pot and also create healthier recipes, I've substituted some healthier ingredients for more traditional ingredients in several of the recipes in this book. Here are some explanations on those ingredients, why I've used them, and some tips on how you can easily swap traditional ingredients back into the recipes should you wish to do so.

BROWN RICE

Almost all the recipes that use rice in this book call for brown rice. Brown rice, along with black and red rice, are whole-grain varieties that have the bran and germ still intact around the grains. The benefits of these varieties are that they're slower to digest, keeping you feeling full longer, and they won't cause blood sugar levels to spike the way other varieties can. While white rice has some nutritional benefits—it's easy to digest; it's low in calories; and some white rice, like basmati, has amino acids, that can help build muscle—these varieties are not as healthy as whole-grain varieties. Brown rice and other whole-grain rice varieties cook for 20 minutes in the Instant Pot, while white rice only cooks for 4 minutes, so you should avoid swapping rice varieties in recipes if possible. If you do choose to swap rice varieties, pay careful attention to the cooking times in the recipes to ensure the rice doesn't come out under- or overcooked.

EGGS

Eggs are used in several recipes in this book, but if you prefer not to eat eggs or are on a low-cholesterol diet and need to avoid the yolks, you can substitute liquid egg whites for whole eggs at a 2:1 ratio. You can also use an egg-free substitute. (The recipes in this book that contain eggs have also been tested with Bob's Red Mill Egg Replacer.)

COTTAGE CHEESE & GREEK YOGURT

A cottage cheese and Greek yogurt mixture is used in several recipes in this book to increase protein content in recipes while reducing fat and calories. When blended, these ingredients also serve as a replacement for more processed ingredients like sour cream, cream cheese, or heavy cream. When cottage cheese and Greek yogurt are blended into a recipe, the tartness from the yogurt and the texture of the cottage cheese usually disappear. Some recipes also use Greek yogurt as a thickener, but when cooked in the Instant Pot, the tart flavor of the Greek yogurt usually disappears.

COCONUT AMINOS

Soy sauce is very high in sodium, so I prefer to use coconut aminos in my recipes as a lower-sodium soy sauce substitute. Coconut aminos contain about 270mg of sodium per tablespoon compared to 960mg per tablespoon for regular soy sauce or about 530mg per tablespoon for reduced-sodium soy sauce. They also contain fewer ingredients than soy sauce, and I promise that you won't taste any coconut in them. If you still prefer to use soy sauce, you can substitute an equal amount of reduced-sodium soy sauce in any recipe that calls for coconut aminos; each recipe mentions reduced-sodium soy sauce as an alternative, if that's what you prefer.

WHOLE WHEAT PASTA

Similar to rice, different types of pasta require different cook times in the Instant Pot. Recipes in this book call for whole wheat pasta, which is healthier than regular white pasta. Using regular pasta in a recipe that calls for whole wheat pasta will likely result in the pasta being overcooked because the cook time for regular pasta is less than it is for whole wheat pasta.

If you still prefer to use regular or gluten-free pasta, you'll want to reduce the cook times accordingly. To adjust cooking times for pasta in the Instant Pot, reduce the cook time listed on the packaging to an even number of minutes, divide that number in half, then subtract two minutes. For example, if the instructions include a 9-minute cook time, reduce it to 8 minutes then divide 8 in half, which gives you 4 minutes, then subtract 2 minutes for a total cook time of 2 minutes.

ALMOND MILK

Dairy products can curdle in the Instant Pot, so many of the recipes in this book that might normally use dairy milk will call for unsweetened almond milk instead. If you don't have almond milk or simply don't like it, you can substitute an equal amount of any other nondairy milk such as oat, soy, cashew, or coconut.

SWEETENERS

The sweeteners used in this book—maple syrup, honey, and coconut sugar—are natural sources of sugar. These sweeteners are less processed than refined white sugar and have a lower glycemic index than white or brown sugar. If you only have white or brown sugar on hand, you can swap 1:1 for coconut sugar or use ¾ cup sugar to 1 cup honey or maple syrup. I'd only recommend substituting the sugars if you're in a pinch, though, because the recipes in this book will taste best with the sweeteners listed, and they'll also be a little healthier.

GROUND MEATS

Certain recipes in this book call for ground beef while others call for leaner ground turkey. You can easily substitute one for the other or you can substitute ground chicken for either, but if you're substituting ground beef in a recipe that calls for sautéing, you'll need to remove the inner pot and drain the rendered fat after cooking. You can also use paper towels to soak up the additional liquid, or you can use a turkey baster to remove it.

STAPLE RECIPES—RICE AND QUINOA

One thing I like to do to help my prep days go faster is to make large batches of "staples" that can be easily added to multiple recipes to make them a meal. Doing this allows me to have them on hand and ready to go whenever they're needed, and it saves me time because having these items precooked and frozen means they only need to be thawed and heated up, and that means the Instant Pot is freed up for other things. All these staples can be cooked, cooled, stored in zipper bags or meal prep containers, and can be refrigerated for 5 to 6 days or frozen for up to 2 months.

QUINOA

PREP: 2 MINUTES
PRESSURE: 1 MINUTE
TOTAL: 13 MINUTES

YIELD: 1 CUP DRY QUINOA EQUALS APPROXIMATELY 4 CUPS COOKED QUINOA
LIQUID: FOR EVERY CUP OF QUINOA, USE 1¼ CUPS OF NONDAIRY LIQUID

1 Spray the inner pot with nonstick cooking spray.

2 Measure out the desired amount of quinoa, rinse and drain, and then add it to the pot.

3 Add 1¼ cups nondairy liquid for every cup of dry quinoa. Close and lock the lid and turn the steam release handle to sealing. Select **Pressure Cook (high)** and set the cook time for **1 minute**. (If you have a **Keep Warm** button, turning it off after cooking will help prevent the rice from sticking to the bottom of the pot.)

4 When the cook time is complete, allow the quinoa to naturally release for 10 minutes, and then quick release the remaining pressure.

Nutrition per ½ cup serving:
CALORIES: 78; **TOTAL FAT:** 2g; **SATURATED FAT:** 1g; **CHOLESTEROL:** 0g; **TOTAL CARBOHYDRATE:** 14g; **SODIUM:** 1mg; **FIBER:** 2g; **PROTEIN:** 3g

WILD RICE

PREP: 2 MINUTES
PRESSURE: 25 MINUTES
TOTAL: 37 MINUTES

YIELD: 1 CUP DRY RICE EQUALS APPROXIMATELY 3 CUPS COOKED RICE
LIQUID: USE EQUAL AMOUNTS OF NONDAIRY LIQUID AND RICE

1 Spray the inner pot with nonstick cooking spray.

2 Measure out the desired amount of rice, rinse and drain, and then add it to the pot.

3 Add an equal amount of nondairy liquid to the pot. Close and lock the lid and turn the steam release handle to sealing. Select **Pressure Cook (high)** and set the cook time for **25 minutes**. (If you have a **Keep Warm** button, turning it off after cooking will help prevent the rice from sticking to the bottom of the pot.)

4 When the cook time is complete, allow the rice to naturally release for 10 minutes, and then quick release the remaining pressure.

Nutrition per ½ cup serving:
CALORIES: 81; **TOTAL FAT:** 1g; **SATURATED FAT:** 0g; **CHOLESTEROL:** 0g; **TOTAL CARBOHYDRATE:** 17g; **SODIUM:** 2mg; **FIBER:** 2g; **PROTEIN:** 3g

You can easily flavor quinoa or rice by using non-dairy milk, low-sodium chicken broth, or vegetable broth in place of water as a cooking liquid. Sometimes, I like to add fresh chopped herbs immediately before serving to add additional flavors to grains.

BROWN, BLACK, OR RED RICE (WHOLE-GRAIN VARIETIES)

 PREP: 2 MINUTES
PRESSURE: 20 MINUTES
TOTAL: 32 MINUTES

 YIELD: 1 CUP DRY RICE EQUALS APPROXIMATELY 2 CUPS COOKED RICE
LIQUID: USE EQUAL AMOUNTS OF NONDAIRY LIQUID AND RICE

1 Spray the inner pot with nonstick cooking spray.

2 Measure out the desired amount of rice, rinse and drain, and then add it to the pot.

3 Add an equal amount of nondairy liquid to the pot. Close and lock the lid and turn the steam release handle to sealing. Select **Pressure Cook (high)** and set the cook time for **20 minutes**. (If you have a **Keep Warm** button, turning it off after cooking will help prevent the rice from sticking to the bottom of the pot.)

4 When the cook time is complete, allow the rice to naturally release for 10 minutes, and then quick release the remaining pressure.

Nutrition per ½ cup serving:
CALORIES: 172; **TOTAL FAT:** 1g; **SATURATED FAT:** 1g; **CHOLESTEROL:** 0g; **TOTAL CARBOHYDRATE:** 36g; **SODIUM:** 2mg; **FIBER:** 2g; **PROTEIN:** 4g

WHITE RICE, BASMATI RICE, OR JASMINE RICE

 PREP: 2 MINUTES
PRESSURE: 4 MINUTES
TOTAL: 16 MINUTES

 YIELD: 1 CUP DRY RICE EQUALS APPROXIMATELY 3 CUPS COOKED RICE
LIQUID: USE EQUAL AMOUNTS OF NONDAIRY LIQUID AND RICE

1 Spray the inner pot with nonstick cooking spray.

2 Measure out the desired amount of rice, rinse and drain, and then add it to the pot.

3 Add an equal amount of nondairy liquid to the pot. Close and lock the lid and turn the steam release handle to sealing. Select **Pressure Cook (high)** and set the cook time for **4 minutes**. (If you have a **Keep Warm** button, turning it off after cooking will help prevent the rice from sticking to the bottom of the pot.)

4 When the cook time is complete, allow the rice to naturally release for 10 minutes, and then quick release the remaining pressure.

Nutrition per ½ cup serving:
CALORIES: 108; **TOTAL FAT:** 1g; **SATURATED FAT:** 1g; **CHOLESTEROL:** 0g; **TOTAL CARBOHYDRATE:** 23g; **SODIUM:** 2mg; **FIBER:** 1g; **PROTEIN:** 3g

STAPLE RECIPES—VEGETABLES

I love cooking large batches of vegetables that can be eaten as sides throughout the week. I typically choose one vegetable per week and then cook up to four cups in the pot at a time. Note that cook times can vary depending on the size of the vegetables and how large you cut them. Many of the recipes in this book include a cooked vegetable, so you may find you're referencing these instructions often.

BROCCOLI

PREP: 2 MINUTES
PRESSURE: 1–2 MINUTES
TOTAL: 3–4 MINUTES

1 Add one cup of water to the bottom of the pot and place the trivet in the pot.

2 Add the rinsed broccoli florets to the pot and on top of the trivet. (It's okay if some fall into the water.)

3 Close and lock the lid and turn the steam release handle to sealing. Select **Pressure Cook (high)** and set the cook time for **1 minute**. When the cook time is complete, quick release the pressure and open the lid. Stick a fork into a floret to see if it's cooked to your liking. If it's cooked to your liking, use a slotted spoon or large tongs to carefully remove the florets from the pot.

4 If you'd prefer the broccoli be cooked a bit more, close the lid again, close the steam release handle, and then set the cook time for **0 (zero) minutes**. The broccoli will continue to cook as the pot pressure builds. Once the pot reaches full pressure, quick release the pressure.

Nutrition per 1 cup serving:
CALORIES: 27; **TOTAL FAT:** 1g; **SATURATED FAT:** 0g; **CHOLESTEROL:** 0g; **TOTAL CARBOHYDRATE:** 6g; **SODIUM:** 26mg; **FIBER:** 3g; **PROTEIN:** 2g

ASPARAGUS

PREP: 1 MINUTE
PRESSURE: 1–2 MINUTES
TOTAL: 2–3 MINUTES

1 Add one cup of water to the bottom of the pot and place the trivet in the pot.

2 Add the rinsed asparagus to the pot and on top of the trivet. (It's okay if some fall into the water.)

3 Close and lock the lid and turn the steam release handle to sealing. Select **Pressure Cook (high)** and set the cook time for **1 minute**. When the cook time is complete, quick release the pressure and open the lid. Stick a fork into a spear to see if it's cooked to your liking. If it's cooked to your liking, use large tongs to carefully remove the asparagus from the pot.

4 If you'd prefer the asparagus be cooked a bit more, close the lid again, close the steam release handle, and then set the cook time for **0 (zero) minutes**. The asparagus will continue to cook as the pot pressure builds. Once the pot reaches full pressure, quick release the pressure.

Nutrition per 1 cup serving:
CALORIES: 27; **TOTAL FAT:** 1g; **SATURATED FAT:** 0g; **CHOLESTEROL:** 0g; **TOTAL CARBOHYDRATE:** 6g; **SODIUM:** 26mg; **FIBER:** 3g; **PROTEIN:** 2g

I like to cook vegetables in the Instant Pot for the minimum amount of time and then check them for doneness. They're less likely to be overcooked, and you can always put the lid back on and cook them for an additional 0 (zero) minutes if they need a little more time.

CAULIFLOWER

PREP: 2 MINUTES
PRESSURE: 2–3 MINUTES
TOTAL: 4–5 MINUTES

1   Add one cup of water to the bottom of the pot and place the trivet in the pot.

2   Add the rinsed cauliflower florets to the pot and on top of the trivet. (It's okay if some fall into the water.)

3   Close and lock the lid and turn the steam release handle to sealing. Select **Pressure Cook (high)** and set the cook time for **2 minutes.** When the cook time is complete, quick release the pressure and open the lid. Stick a fork into a floret to see if it's cooked to your liking. If it's cooked to your liking, use a slotted spoon or large tongs to carefully remove the florets from the pot.

4   If you'd prefer the cauliflower be cooked a bit more, close the lid again, close the steam release handle, and then set the cook time for **0 (zero) minutes.** The cauliflower will continue to cook as the pot pressure builds. Once the pot reaches full pressure, quick release the pressure.

Nutrition per 1 cup serving:
CALORIES: 25; **TOTAL FAT:** 1g; **SATURATED FAT:** 0g; **CHOLESTEROL:** 0g; **TOTAL CARBOHYDRATE:** 5g; **SODIUM:** 30mg; **FIBER:** 3g; **PROTEIN:** 2g

GREEN BEANS

PREP: 5 MINUTES
PRESSURE: 1–2 MINUTES
TOTAL: 6–7 MINUTES

1   Add one cup of water to the bottom of the pot and place the trivet in the pot.

2   Add the rinsed and trimmed green beans to the pot and on top of the trivet. (It's okay if some fall into the water.)

3   Close and lock the lid and turn the steam release handle to sealing. Select **Pressure Cook (high)** and set the cook time for **1 minute.** When the cook time is complete, quick release the pressure and open the lid. Stick a fork into a green bean to see if it's cooked to your liking. If it's cooked to your liking, use large tongs to carefully remove the green beans from the pot.

4   If you'd prefer the green beans be cooked a bit more, close the lid again, close the steam release handle, and then set the cook time for **0 (zero) minutes.** The beans will continue to cook as the pot pressure builds. Once the pot reaches full pressure, quick release the pressure.

Nutrition per 1 cup serving:
CALORIES: 31; **TOTAL FAT:** 1g; **SATURATED FAT:** 0g; **CHOLESTEROL:** 0g; **TOTAL CARBOHYDRATE:** 7g; **SODIUM:** 6mg; **FIBER:** 4g; **PROTEIN:** 2g

WEEK ONE
PREP PLAN

WEEK ONE PREP PLAN

This week's meals include a perfect balance of whole-grain comfort foods like Apple Cinnamon Baked Oatmeal and Macaroni and Cheese, along with vegetable-packed recipes like Beef Fajita Bowls and Minestrone Soup. Meal prepping these healthy recipes will help you stay on track all week long!

If desired, you can substitute one or more of the alternate recipes for the primary recipes in a plan. I often will make one of the alternate recipes during a prep day and freeze it in single-serving containers to thaw and reheat later. In order to integrate alternate recipes into your prep plan, reference the meal planning tips on pages 16 and 17 to determine how to swap alternate recipes into your prep session.

PREP PLAN YIELDS

APPLE CINNAMON BAKED OATMEAL

×8

BEEF FAJITA BOWLS

×8

RECICPES

PRIMARY

- Apple Cinnamon Baked Oatmeal (p. 36)
- Beef Fajita Bowls (p. 39)
- Macaroni and Cheese (p. 40)
- Minestrone Soup (p. 43)

ALTERNATE

- Fajita Breakfast Casserole (p. 44)
- Chicken Burrito Bowls (p. 45)
- Mexican Meatloaf with Potatoes and Vegetables (p. 46)
- Chocolate Chip Brownies (p. 47)

MACARONI & CHEESE

×8

MINESTRONE SOUP

×8

SHOPPING LIST

PRODUCE

- ○ 2 medium red onions
- ○ 1 bunch celery
- ○ 5 large carrots
- ○ 3 medium zucchini
- ○ 2 tsp minced fresh garlic
- ○ 1-inch piece fresh ginger root
- ○ 1 cup baby leaf spinach (optional)
- ○ 4 medium bell peppers, any color
- ○ 2 medium apples, any variety (Honeycrisp recommended)
- ○ 2 mediums heads broccoli

MEAT & DAIRY

- ○ 3lb (1.35kg) flank steak
- ○ 3 tbsp butter
- ○ 7oz (200g) container, plain, low-fat Greek yogurt
- ○ 2 cups shredded Monterey Jack cheese
- ○ 1 cup shredded cheddar cheese
- ○ 1 cup shredded mozzarella
- ○ 10 eggs

PANTRY & DRY GOODS

- ○ 3⅓ cups plain, unsweetened almond milk
- ○ 2 x 16oz (455g) boxes whole wheat elbow macaroni
- ○ ½ cup canned dark red kidney beans
- ○ Nonstick cooking spray
- ○ ½ cup canned cannellini beans
- ○ 14.5oz (410g) can low-sodium diced tomatoes
- ○ 8 cups low-sodium vegetable broth
- ○ 5 cups rolled oats
- ○ 5 tbsp maple syrup
- ○ 32oz (905g) bag dry brown rice
- ○ 5 tsp vanilla extract
- ○ 2½ tsp baking powder
- ○ 6 tbsp coconut aminos or reduced-sodium soy sauce
- ○ 1 tsp rice vinegar
- ○ 3 tbsp honey

SPICES & SEASONINGS

- ○ 1½ tsp dried oregano
- ○ 1½ tsp salt
- ○ 2 tsp dried basil
- ○ 1 tsp dried sage
- ○ 1 tsp dried parsley
- ○ 2 bay leaves
- ○ 4 tsp ground cinnamon

EQUIPMENT

- ○ 6qt Instant Pot and trivet
- ○ 26 meal prep containers
- ○ 8 meal prep bowls (for soup)
- ○ 7in round baking pan or oven-safe dish
- ○ Large mixing bowl
- ○ Measuring cups
- ○ Measuring spoons
- ○ Chef's knife
- ○ Paring knife
- ○ Microplaner
- ○ Cutting board
- ○ Strainer
- ○ Large spatula or spoon
- ○ Oven mitts

PREP PLAN

1 Follow step 1 for the **Beef Fajita Bowls (p. 39)**. Spray the inner pot with nonstick cooking spray, add the rice and water to the pot, and cook according to the instructions (p. 27).

2 While the rice is cooking, cut the vegetables for **Minestrone Soup (p. 43)** and combine them in a large bowl. Add the spices on top of the vegetables, then stir to combine. Set aside.

3 When the rice has finished cooking, allow a 10-minute natural pressure release before quick releasing the remaining pressure, then divide ½-cup servings into 8 meal prep containers.

4 Wash the inner pot and spray with nonstick cooking spray. Follow steps 2–4 to cook the minestrone soup.

5 While the soup is cooking, begin making the **Apple Cinnamon Baked Oatmeal (p. 36)** by dicing the apples and combining them in a large bowl with the other ingredients.

6 When the soup is done cooking, allow it to cool for a few minutes, then remove the bay leaves and divide equal-sized portions into 8 meal prep containers. Transfer the containers to the refrigerator to complete the recipe.

7 Wash the inner pot and spray it with nonstick cooking spray. Add the oatmeal mixture to the pot and follow steps 1, 3, and 4 to cook the oatmeal.

8 While the oatmeal is cooking, slice the peppers, onions, and steak for the fajita bowls. Prepare the marinade in a large bowl and add the steak to the bowl to marinate while the oatmeal finishes cooking.

9 When the cook time for the oatmeal is complete, quick release the pressure and divide 1-cup servings into 8 meal prep containers. Place the containers in the refrigerator to complete the recipe.

10 Wash the inner pot and spray with nonstick cooking spray. Add the steak and marinade to the pot and follow step 5 to cook the steak.

11 While the steak is cooking, wash and cut the broccoli for the fajita bowls.

12 When the steak is done cooking, follow step 6 to cook the onions and peppers wiht the steak.

13 After the steak, peppers, and onions are cooked, slice the steak and divide equal amounts of the steak, peppers, and onions into the containers with the rice.

14 Wash the inner pot and add 1 cup of water to the pot. Place the trivet in the pot and place the broccoli on the trivet. Cook according to the instructions (p. 28).

15 When the broccoli is done cooking, quick release the pressure and divide the broccoli into the containers for the fajita bowls. Seal the containers and transfer them to the fridge to complete the recipe.

16 Wash the inner pot and spray it with nonstick cooking spray. Follow steps 1 and 2 for the **Macaroni and Cheese (p. 40)** by combining the pasta, water, and salt in the pot. Cook according to instructions.

17 While the pasta is cooking, prepare the remaining ingredients for the macaroni and cheese.

18 After the pasta is finished cooking, drain, then follow step 5 to add the remaining ingredients. Allow the macaroni and cheese to cool for 5 minutes and then divide it into 8 meal prep containers. Place the containers in the fridge to complete the recipe.

gf **df**

SERVES: 8
SERVING SIZE: 1 CUP

PREP: 15 MINUTES
PRESSURE: 50 MINUTES
TOTAL: 1 HOUR 5 MINUTES

SETTINGS: PRESSURE COOK
RELEASE: QUICK

4 cups rolled oats

3⅓ cups plain, unsweetened almond milk

2 tsp baking powder

1 tbsp ground cinnamon

4 tsp vanilla extract

¼ cup maple syrup

8 eggs

2 medium apples, peeled and diced (I love using Honeycrisp apples for this recipe.)

APPLE CINNAMON BAKED OATMEAL

This hearty breakfast dish is thicker than traditional oatmeal—almost like a muffin. If desired, you can top with maple syrup, peanut butter, or your favorite fresh fruit!

1   Add 1½ cups of water to the inner pot. Spray the inside of a 7-inch round baking pan or oven-safe dish with nonstick cooking spray. Set aside.

2   In a large bowl, combine the oats, almond milk, baking powder, cinnamon, vanilla extract, maple syrup, eggs, and diced apples. Stir until the eggs are blended and all ingredients are well combined.

3   Add the oatmeal mixture to the prepared baking pan and cover the pan with aluminum foil. Place the pot on the trivet and grasp the handles to carefully lower the dish into the pot.

4   Close and lock the lid, then turn the steam release handle to sealing. Select **Pressure Cook (high)** and set the cook time for **40 minutes**. When the cook time is complete, quick release the pressure and remove the lid. Use oven mitts to grasp the trivet handles and carefully lift the dish out of the pot.

5   Divide 1-cup servings into 8 meal prep containers. Store in the fridge for up to 6 days or freeze for up to 2 months.

Reheating: Microwave each thawed serving for 1½ to 2 minutes. (If the oatmeal seems dry after reheating, add a few teaspoons of almond milk and stir before serving.)

tip *If your dish is larger than the trivet, you can make a foil sling to lower the dish into the pot.*

Nutrition per serving:
CALORIES: 289; **TOTAL FAT:** 8g; **SATURATED FAT:** 2g; **CHOLESTEROL:** 164mg; **SODIUM:** 203mg; **TOTAL CARBOHYDRATE:** 42g; **FIBER:** 5g; **PROTEIN:** 11g

MINESTRONE SOUP

This satisfying soup features hearty vegetables and whole-grain pasta cooked in a seasoned vegetable broth. This soup is easy to freeze and perfect for prepping!

1 Spray the bottom of the inner pot with nonstick cooking spray. Select **Sauté**.

2 Add the onions, celery, carrots, and zucchini. Sprinkle in the oregano, salt, basil, sage, garlic, and parsley, then stir to combine. Sauté the ingredients for 3–4 minutes or until the onions are translucent and the vegetables are fragrant, then turn off the pot.

3 Add the pasta, kidney beans, cannellini beans, diced tomatoes, vegetable broth. Stir to combine and then add the bay leaves.

4 Close and lock the lid, then turn the steam release handle to sealing. Select **Pressure Cook (high)** and set the cook time for **4 minutes**.

5 When the cook time is complete, quick release the pressure, remove the bay leaves, then add the spinach (if using) and stir. Close the lid for an additional 3–5 minutes to allow the spinach to cook.

6 Divide 1½-cup portions into 8 meal prep containers. Store in the fridge for up to 5 days or freeze for up to 2 months.

Reheating: Microwave each thawed serving for 2 to 2½ minutes.

SERVES: 8
SERVING SIZE: 1½ CUPS

PREP: 20 MINUTES
PRESSURE: 4 MINUTES
TOTAL: 24 MINUTES

SETTINGS: SAUTÉ/PRESSURE COOK
RELEASE: QUICK

1 cup diced red onion

2½ cups diced celery

2½ cups diced carrots

2 cups diced zucchini

1½ tsp dried oregano

½ tsp salt

2 tsp dried basil

1 tsp dried sage

2 tsp minced fresh garlic

1 tsp dried parsley

1 cup whole wheat elbow macaroni (or any other short noodle)

½ cup canned dark red kidney beans, drained

½ cup canned cannellini beans, drained

14.5oz (410g) can low-sodium diced tomatoes

8 cups low-sodium vegetable broth

2 bay leaves

1 cup chopped fresh spinach (optional)

tip *To make this recipe gluten-free, replace the whole wheat pasta with gluten-free pasta, then reduce the cook time listed on the pasta packaging by half.*

Nutrition per serving:
CALORIES: 147; **TOTAL FAT:** 1g; **SATURATED FAT:** 1g; **CHOLESTEROL:** 0mg; **SODIUM:** 66mg; **TOTAL CARBOHYDRATE:** 31g; **FIBER:** 5g; **PROTEIN:** 7g

SERVES: 2
SERVING SIZE: 1 CUP VEGETABLES
& 2 EGGS

 PREP: 10 MINUTES
PRESSURE: 3 MINUTES
TOTAL: 13 MINUTES

 SETTINGS: SAUTÉ/PRESSURE COOK
RELEASE: QUICK

---

1 tsp olive oil

½ cup sliced red onions

1½ cups sliced bell peppers
(any color)

⅛ tsp chili powder

⅛ tsp smoked paprika

⅛ tsp onion powder

⅛ tsp garlic powder

⅛ tsp cumin

⅛ tsp cayenne pepper (optional)

4 eggs

4 tbsp chopped fresh cilantro

1 small lime, cut in half and seeded

½ medium avocado, sliced

tip *If your dish is larger than the trivet, you can make a foil sling to lower the dish into the pot.*

FAJITA BREAKFAST CASSEROLE

This simple, yet flavorful, dish is a healthy, low-carb way to begin your day. It also makes a great last-minute dinner option for those nights when you don't have a lot of time to cook!

1 Select **Sauté** and add the olive oil to the inner pot.

2 When the oil is hot, add the onions, bell peppers, chili powder, smoked paprika, onion powder, garlic powder, cumin, and cayenne pepper (if using). Sauté for 4 minutes or until the onions become slightly translucent, then turn off the pot.

3 Spray a 7-inch round baking pan or oven-safe dish with nonstick cooking spray. Transfer the onions and peppers to the pan.

4 Gently crack the eggs over the top of the onions and peppers, being careful to keep the yolks intact. Loosely cover the dish with aluminum foil.

5 Add 1 cup of water to the inner pot. Place the dish on the trivet, then grasp the trivet handles to lower the dish into the pot..

6 Close and lock the lid, then turn the steam release handle to sealing. Select **Pressure Cook (high)** and set the cook time for **3 minutes**. When the cook time is complete, quick release the pressure and remove the lid. Use oven mitts to grasp the trivet handles and carefully lift the dish out of the pot.

7 Transfer 1 cup of the vegetables and 2 eggs to each of 2 meal prep containers. Garnish each serving with 2 tablespoons of the cilantro, 1 lime half, and ½ of the sliced avocado. Store in the fridge for up to 6 days. (This recipe does not freeze well.)

Reheating: Microwave each thawed serving for 30 seconds to 1 minute.

Nutrition per serving:
CALORIES: 277; **TOTAL FAT:** 18g; **SATURATED FAT:** 4g; **CHOLESTEROL:** 327mg; **SODIUM:** 135mg; **TOTAL CARBOHYDRATE:** 15g; **FIBER:** 6g; **PROTEIN:** 14g

CHICKEN BURRITO BOWLS

Using frozen chicken and dry rice and beans helps make this a super-easy prep recipe. If desired, top with shredded romaine, shredded cheddar cheese, sliced avocado, or salsa.

 SERVES: 8
SERVING SIZE: ⅔ CUP

 PREP: 5 MINUTES
PRESSURE: 25 MINUTES
TOTAL: 30 MINUTES

 SETTINGS: PRESSURE COOK
RELEASE: QUICK RELEASE

1 Place the chicken breasts flat in the inner pot, but do not stack. (If the chicken breasts are stacked, they won't cook properly.) Add the brown rice, black beans, tomatoes, garlic, crushed red pepper, cayenne pepper, lime juice, cilantro, and chicken stock.

2 Close and lock the lid, then turn the steam release handle to sealing. Select **Pressure Cook (high)** and set the cook time for **25 minutes.** When the cook time is complete, quick release the pressure and remove the lid.

3 Transfer the chicken to a large bowl and use two forks to shred. (Alternatively, you can use a hand mixer.)

4 Return the chicken to the inner pot, mix well, and then divide ⅔-cup servings into 8 meal prep containers. Store in the fridge for up to 6 days or freeze for up to 2 months.

Reheating: Microwave each thawed serving for 1 to 1½ minutes.

2lb (905g) frozen chicken breasts

⅔ cup uncooked brown rice, rinsed

⅔ cup uncooked black beans

2 x 15oz (425g) cans diced tomatoes, drained

10 cloves garlic, minced

3 tsp crushed red pepper

3 tsp cayenne pepper

Juice of one lime

5 tbsp chopped fresh cilantro

2 cups chicken stock

tip *If the beans are not soft enough for your liking, close the lid and set the timer for 0 (zero) minutes, and then allow the pressure to release naturally. This will cook the beans a bit more and give them a slightly softer texture.*

Nutrition per serving:
CALORIES: 227; **TOTAL FAT:** 4g; **SATURATED FAT:** 1g; **CHOLESTEROL:** 73mg; **SODIUM:** 216mg; **TOTAL CARBOHYDRATE:** 19g; **FIBER:** 3g; **PROTEIN:** 28g

SERVES: 6
SERVING SIZE: ⅙ OF MEATLOAF,
⅓ CUP POTATOES, ¼ CUP CARROTS
& ABOUT 12 GREEN BEANS

PREP: 10 MINUTES
PRESSURE: 17 MINUTES
TOTAL: 27 MINUTES

SETTINGS: PRESSURE COOK
RELEASE: QUICK

2 cups baby potatoes, washed

1lb (455g) ground turkey

1 cup canned corn and peppers, drained

10oz (285g) can diced tomatoes and green chilies, drained

1 egg

1 medium red onion, chopped (about ¾ cup)

4oz (115g) can green jalapeños (optional)

1 tbsp chili powder

1 tsp cumin

2 tsp minced fresh garlic

1 tsp smoked paprika

½ tsp crushed red pepper (optional)

5 large carrots, peeled and sliced into thirds

1lb (455g) fresh green beans, washed and trimmed

⅔ cup shredded cheddar jack cheese (for topping)

MEXICAN MEATLOAF
with Potatoes and Vegetables

This spicy twist on a traditional meatloaf dinner is delicious and family friendly! Cooking this entire meal in one pot is a definite time saver.

1 Place the trivet in the inner pot and add 2 cups of water. Place the potatoes on the trivet.

2 Combine the ground turkey, corn and peppers, tomatoes and chilies, egg, onions, and jalapeños (if using) in a medium bowl. Sprinkle the chili powder, cumin, garlic, paprika, and crushed red pepper (if using) over the top. Stir until well combined.

3 Use a 12-inch sheet of aluminum foil to create a "D"-shaped foil bowl for the meatloaf that is approximately 4 inches deep. Spray the inside of the bowl with nonstick cooking spray, transfer the meatloaf mixture to the bowl, and place the bowl on top of the potatoes and off to one side of the pot. Make a second "D"-shaped foil bowl, spray the bowl with nonstick cooking spray, place the carrots in the bowl and place the bowl on top of the potatoes and next to the meatloaf bowl.

4 Close and lock the lid, then turn the steam release handle to sealing. Select **Pressure Cook (high)** and set the cook time for **15 minutes**.

5 While the meatloaf, potatoes, and carrots are cooking, make another foil bowl that is large enough to span the entire circumference of the inner pot for the green beans. Spray the bowl with nonstick cooking spray and transfer the green beans to the bowl.

6 Once the cook time for the meatloaf, potatoes, and carrots is complete, quick release the pressure and remove the lid. Place the green bean bowl on top of the meatloaf and carrots. Close the lid, keeping the steam release handle turned to venting so the lid goes on easier, then turn the steam release handle to sealing. Select **Pressure Cook (high)** and set the cook time for **2 minutes**.

7 When the cook time is complete, quick release the pressure and carefully remove the green beans, meatloaf, carrots, and potatoes from the pot. Cut the meatloaf into 6 equal-sized slices and transfer the slices to meal prep containers. Garnish each serving with equal amounts of shredded cheese, then add equal amounts of the potatoes, carrots, and green beans to each container. Store in the fridge for up to 4 days or freeze for up to 2 months.

Reheating: Microwave each thawed serving for 1½ to 2 minutes.

Nutrition per serving:
CALORIES: 259; **TOTAL FAT:** 8g; **SATURATED FAT:** 2g; **CHOLESTEROL:** 59mg; **SODIUM:** 177mg; **TOTAL CARBOHYDRATE:** 28g; **FIBER:** 6g; **PROTEIN:** 22g

CHOCOLATE CHIP BROWNIES

Fudgy and rich, these brownies are the perfect ending to a healthy meal! The dark chocolate in this recipe is high in antioxidants and so rich that just a small slice will satisfy your sweet cravings.

SERVES: 12
SERVING SIZE: 1 BROWNIE

PREP: 10 MINUTES
PRESSURE: 50 MINUTES
TOTAL: 1 HOUR 15 MINUTES

SETTINGS: PRESSURE COOK
RELEASE: NATURAL/QUICK

1½ cups dark chocolate chips, divided

¼ cup coconut oil

4 eggs

1 cup coconut crystals (also called coconut sugar)

1 tbsp vanilla extract

½ tsp almond extract

¼ tsp sea salt

½ tsp powdered stevia

½ cup almond flour

2 tbsp coconut flour

1 Place the trivet in the inner pot and add 2 cups of water. Spray the inside of a 7-inch round baking pan or oven-safe dish with nonstick cooking spray. Set aside.

2 Place 1 cup of the chocolate chips in a large glass bowl. Microwave on high for 2–3 minutes, stirring every 30 seconds, until the chocolate is completely melted, then add the coconut oil and stir until the oil is completely dissolved.

3 Add the eggs, coconut crystals, vanilla extract, almond extract, sea salt, and stevia to the bowl with the chocolate. Use a handheld mixer or spatula to mix until combined, then add the almond flour and coconut flour and continue mixing until the ingredients are well combined.

4 Add the remaining ½ cup of chocolate chips to the bowl and use a spatula to fold them into the batter. Add the batter to the prepared dish and cover with foil. Place the dish on the trivet, then grasp the trivet handles to lower the dish into the pot..

5 Close and lock the lid, then turn the steam release handle to sealing. Select **Pressure Cook (high)** and set the cook time for **50 minutes**. When the cook time is complete, let the pressure release naturally for 15 minutes, then quick release the remaining pressure and remove the lid. Use oven mitts to grasp the trivet handles and carefully lift the dish out of the pot.

6 Cut the cooled brownies into 12 equal-sized servings and transfer them to meal prep containers. Store in the fridge for up to 6 days or freeze for up to 2 months.

tip *If your dish is larger than the trivet, you can make a foil sling to lower the dish into the pot.*

Nutrition per serving:
CALORIES: 195; **TOTAL FAT:** 14g; **SATURATED FAT:** 11g; **CHOLESTEROL:** 1mg; **SODIUM:** 27mg; **TOTAL CARBOHYDRATE:** 14g; **FIBER:** 2g; **PROTEIN:** 3g

WEEK TWO
PREP PLAN

WEEK TWO PREP PLAN

Meals for this week include savory southwestern flavors in a Light & Fluffy Egg Casserole, Southwest Stuffed Peppers, Carne Asada Street Taco Bowls, and sweet and savory Teriyaki Meatball Bowls. Note that you'll be making two batches of the Southwest Stuffed Peppers—one during your prep day and a second mid-week.

If desired, you can substitute one or more of the alternate recipes for the primary recipes in a plan. I often will make one of the alternate recipes during a prep day and freeze it in single-serving containers to thaw and reheat later. In order to integrate alternate recipes into your prep plan, reference the meal planning tips on pages 16 and 17 to determine how to swap alternate recipes into your prep session.

PREP PLAN YIELDS

LIGHT & FLUFFY EGG CASSEROLE

×10

SOUTHWEST STUFFED PEPPERS

×8

RECISPES

PRIMARY

- Light & Fluffy Egg Casserole (p. 54)
- Southwest Stuffed Peppers (p. 57)
- Carne Asada Street Taco Bowls (p. 58)
- Teriyaki Meatball Bowls (p. 61)

ALTERNATE

- Mini Egg Scrambles (p. 62)
- Spicy Enchilada Casserole (p. 63)
- Orange Chicken (p. 64)
- Easy Lava Cake Bites (p. 65)

CARNE ASADA STREET TACO BOWLS

×8

TERIYAKI MEATBALL BOWLS

×7

SHOPPING LIST

PRODUCE

- 9 medium bell peppers, 1 red or green, then your choice of color
- 2 x 8oz (225g) containers white button or baby Portobello mushrooms
- 2 medium zucchinis
- 2 medium onions, any variety
- 1 fresh green chile
- 1 jalapeño pepper
- 1 medium lime
- 1 medium Valencia orange
- 1 bunch green onions
- 2 large heads cauliflower (about 8 cups)
- 2 large heads broccoli (about 7 cups)
- 1 small piece fresh ginger root
- 5 cloves garlic

MEAT & DAIRY

- 3½lb (1.6kg) ground turkey
- 3lb (1.35kg) flank steak
- 1½ cups shredded cheddar cheese
- 1 cup shredded Cheddar jack cheese
- 10 eggs
- 2 x 7oz (200g) containers 2% cottage cheese
- 2 x 7oz (200g) containers plain 2% Greek yogurt

PANTRY & DRY GOODS

- 1 cup corn (frozen or canned)
- 14oz (395g) can black beans
- 20oz (565g) can packed-in-juice crushed pineapple
- 32oz (905g) bag dry brown rice
- ¼ cup plus 1 tsp white vinegar
- 8 tbsp plus 1 tsp coconut aminos
- 4 tsp olive oil
- ½ cup rolled oats
- 2 tbsp honey
- Nonstick cooking spray

SPICES & SEASONINGS

- 3 tbsp plus 1 tsp chili powder
- 2 tsp cayenne pepper (optional)
- 1 tsp smoked paprika
- 3 tsp cumin
- 3 tsp dried oregano
- ¾ tsp salt
- ½ tsp freshly ground black pepper
- 2 tsp garlic powder
- 2 tsp onion powder

EQUIPMENT

- 6qt Instant Pot and trivet
- 33 meal prep containers
- 7in round baking pan or oven-safe dish
- Measuring cups
- Measuring spoons
- 2 large bowls
- Medium bowl
- Large spoon or spatula
- Slotted spoon
- Large tongs
- Chef's knife
- Cutting board
- Large pan
- Aluminum foil

PREP PLAN

1 Spray the inner pot with nonstick cooking spray and add 4 cups of dry brown rice plus 4 cups of water to the pot. Follow the instructions for cooking brown rice (p. 27).

2 While the rice is cooking, cut the vegetables for two batches of the **Southwest Stuffed Peppers (p. 57)**. (For the peppers, only cut the tops off of four. Wash and dry the remaining peppers and transfer them to the refrigerator for the midweek prep.) Set aside.

3 Wash and cut the cauliflower for the **Carne Asada Street Taco Bowls (p. 58)** into small florets, then set aside.

4 Follow step 2 to assemble the meatball ingredients for the **Teriyaki Meatball Bowls (p. 61)**. Spray two egg bite molds with nonstick cooking spray and fill the molds with the meatball mixture. Cover the molds with foil and place them in the refrigerator until ready to cook.

5 Dice the vegetables for the **Light & Fluffy Egg Casserole (p. 54)** and combine them in a large bowl. Set aside.

6 When the rice is done cooking, reserve 1 cup for the stuffed pepper mixture, and then divide the remaining rice equally between 15 meal prep containers. Set the containers aside. Wash the inner pot.

7 Follow steps 2 and 4 to sauté the filling for the stuffed peppers. When the mixture is done cooking, follow step 5 to combine the turkey mixture with the other ingredients. Divide the mixture in half, use one half to stuff four of the peppers and then transfer the remaining half to a zipper lock freezer bag and add ½ cup of shredded cheese to the bag. Flatten the bag so it freezes in a thin single layer and then transfer it to the freezer.

8 Place the trivet in the pot and add 1 cup of water. Place the stuffed peppers on the trivet and top with the remaining cheese. Follow steps 7 and 8 to cook the peppers.

9 While the peppers are cooking, follow steps 2 and 3 to combine the ingredients for the breakfast casserole.

10 When the cook time for the stuffed peppers is complete, quick release the pressure and remove the lid. Use tongs to transfer the peppers to 4 meal prep containers. Place the containers in the fridge to complete the recipe.

11 Rinse the inner pot and add the trivet back to the pot along with 1 cup of water. Follow steps 1 and 4 to cook the breakfast casserole.

12 While the breakfast casserole is cooking, follow step 2 to make the marinade for the street taco bowls. Place the steak in the marinade and set aside. Chop the cilantro and onions for the street taco bowls.

13 Follow step 5 to prepare the glaze for the teriyaki meatball bowls. Wash and cut the broccoli for the meatball bowls. Set aside.

14 When the breakfast casserole is done cooking, remove it from the pot and remove the foil. Set the casserole aside to cool.

15 Wash the inner pot and place the trivet in the pot along with ½ cup of water. Add the steak and marinade for the street taco bowls and follow step 5 to cook the steak. Once the steak is partially cooked, follow step 6 to cut the steak, then follow step 7 to finish cooking the steak. Transfer it to the 8 meal prep containers with the rice.

16 Rinse the inner pot and add 1 cup of water along with the trivet. Remove the egg bite molds with the meatballs from the fridge and follow steps 3 and 4 to cook the meatballs.

17 While the meatballs are cooking, cut the casserole into 10 servings and transfer them to meal prep containers to complete the recipe.

18 When the meatballs are done cooking, wash the inner pot and place the trivet in the pot. Add 1 cup of water to the pot and place the cauliflower florets on the trivet. Cook according to instructions (p. 29).

19 When the cauliflower is finished cooking, divide it equally across the 8 containers for the taco bowls. Top with the onions and cilantro, then transfer the containers to the fridge to complete the recipe.

20 Rinse the inner pot and place the trivet in the pot along with 1 cup of water. Add the broccoli and follow the instructions for cooking (p. 28).

21 When the broccoli is finished cooking, divide it evenly across the 7 meal prep containers for the teriyaki meatball bowls.

22 Follow steps 7 and 8 to remove the meatballs from the molds. Place them in the meal prep containers and transfer the containers to the fridge to complete the recipe.

Midweek prep:

1 Remove the turkey and cheese mixture from the freezer and allow to thaw in the refrigerator.

2 Follow steps 6–9 to cook the remaining stuffed peppers.

SERVES: 10
SERVING SIZE: 1 SLICE

PREP: 10 MINUTES
PRESSURE: 45 MINUTES
TOTAL: 1 HOUR 5 MINUTES

SETTINGS: PRESSURE COOK
RELEASE: NATURAL

8 eggs

1 cup 2% cottage cheese

1 cup plain 2% Greek yogurt

½ cup diced onion (any variety)

½ cup diced red or green bell peppers

¼ cup diced fresh green chiles

⅛ cup diced jalapeño peppers

¼ tsp salt

1½ cups shredded cheddar cheese

tip *If desired, add 1 cup of cooked, diced bacon in step 3.*

LIGHT & FLUFFY EGG CASSEROLE

Onions and peppers are perfect complements to the light and fluffy texture of this recipe. The texture of this casserole is reminiscent of sous-vide egg bites.

1 Add 1 cup of water to the bottom of the inner pot. Spray a 7-inch round baking pan or oven-safe dish with nonstick cooking spray. Set aside.

2 Combine the eggs, cottage cheese, and Greek yogurt in a food processor or blender. Process on low until smooth, about 1 minute.

3 Transfer the egg mixture to a large bowl, then add the onions, bell peppers, green chilies, jalapeños, and salt. Stir until just combined, but do not over mix. Pour the mixture into the prepared baking pan and then sprinkle the cheddar cheese over the top. (The mixture may appear thin, but this is normal.) Tightly cover the dish with aluminum foil.

4 Place the dish on the trivet and grasp the trivet handles to carefully lower the dish into the pot. Close and lock the lid, then turn the steam release handle to sealing. Select **Pressure Cook (high)** and set the cook time for **45 minutes**.

5 When the cook time is complete, allow the pressure to release naturally, then use oven mitts to carefully grasp the trivet handles and remove the dish from the pot. Carefully remove the foil from the dish and let the casserole cool to room temperature. (Note that the casserole will fall as it cools.)

6 Cut the cooled casserole into 10 equal slices and transfer them to meal prep containers. Store in the fridge for up to 4 days. (This recipe does not freeze well.)

Reheating: Microwave each thawed serving for 45 seconds to 1 minute.

Nutrition per serving:
CALORIES: 159; **TOTAL FAT:** 10g; **SATURATED FAT:** 5g; **CHOLESTEROL:** 151mg; **SODIUM:** 328mg; **TOTAL CARBOHYDRATE:** 4g; **FIBER:** 1g; **PROTEIN:** 14g

SOUTHWEST STUFFED PEPPERS

This flavorful, colorful meal is satisfying and filled with traditional southwestern flavors. The extra vegetables help make this recipe a healthy favorite in our house.

SERVES: 4
SERVING SIZE: 1 PEPPER

PREP: 15 MINUTES
PRESSURE: 25 MINUTES
TOTAL: 50 MINUTES

SETTINGS: SAUTÉ/PRESSURE COOK
RELEASE: QUICK

1 Add the water and rice to the pot, then follow the instructions for cooking brown rice (p. 27).

2 Rinse and dry the inner pot. Select **Sauté** and spray the inner pot with nonstick cooking spray.

3 While the pot is heating up, slice the tops off of the bell peppers and use a spoon to scoop out the seeds and membranes. Set the shells aside, discard the seeds and membranes, then remove the stems and dice the remaining flesh from the tops. Set aside.

4 When the pot is hot, add the ground turkey, diced peppers, garlic, chili powder, cayenne pepper (if using), smoked paprika, cumin, oregano, salt, black pepper, mushrooms, zucchini, and onions. Stir to combine. Sauté until the turkey is browned and the spices are fragrant, about 10 minutes.

5 When the turkey is browned and the diced peppers are soft, use a slotted spoon to transfer the mixture to a medium bowl. Add the corn, black beans, cooked rice, and ⅓ cup of the cheese to the turkey mixture. Mix well.

6 Rinse and dry the inner pot and place it back in the base. Place the trivet in the pot and add one cup of water.

7 Using a serving spoon, stuff each pepper to the top with the filling, then place the stuffed peppers on the trivet. (It's okay if the peppers are touching each other or the sides of the pot.) Top the peppers with the remaining cheese.

8 Close and lock the lid, then turn the steam release handle to sealing. Select **Pressure Cook (high)** and set the cook time for **5 minutes**. When the cook time is complete, quick release the pressure and remove the lid.

9 Use tongs to carefully transfer the peppers to 4 meal prep containers. Store in the fridge for up to 6 days or freeze for up to 2 months.

Reheating: Microwave each thawed serving for 2 to 2½ minutes.

1 cup uncooked brown rice

1 cup water

4 medium bell peppers (any color)

1lb (450g) ground turkey

1 tsp minced garlic

2 tsp chili powder

1 tsp cayenne pepper (optional)

½ tsp smoked paprika

½ tsp cumin

½ tsp dried oregano

¼ tsp salt

¼ tsp black pepper

1 cup chopped white button or baby Portobello mushrooms

1 cup chopped zucchini

½ cup chopped onion (any variety)

½ cup corn (frozen or canned)

½ cup canned black beans, drained

½ cup shredded cheddar cheese, divided

tip *To make this recipe vegetarian, replace the ground turkey with 2 cups chopped mushrooms.*

Nutrition per serving:
CALORIES: 491; **TOTAL FAT:** 16g; **SATURATED FAT:** 6g; **CHOLESTEROL:** 99mg; **SODIUM:** 260mg; **TOTAL CARBOHYDRATE:** 55g; **FIBER:** 7g; **PROTEIN:** 32g

SERVES: 8
SERVING SIZE: ¾ CUP STEAK,
½ CUP RICE, & 1 CUP CAULIFLOWER

 PREP: 25 MINUTES
PRESSURE: 30 MINUTES
TOTAL: 1 HOUR

 SETTINGS: PRESSURE COOK/SAUTÉ
RELEASE: QUICK

---

2 cups uncooked brown rice

2 cups water (for the rice)

3lb (1.35kg) flank steak

2 large cauliflower heads, chopped into florets

½ cup water (for the steak)

FOR THE MARINADE

¼ cup white vinegar

¼ cup coconut aminos or reduced-sodium soy sauce

4 tsp olive oil

Juice of 1 medium lime

Juice of 1 medium Valencia orange

2 tsp garlic powder

2 tbsp chili powder

2 tsp dried oregano

2 tsp ground cumin

2 tsp onion powder

FOR TOPPING

1 bunch cilantro, chopped

1 medium onion, chopped

CARNE ASADA STREET TACO BOWLS

Traditional carne asada street tacos are a true treat! These bowls take a slightly more prep-friendly approach for the preparation, but they still feature traditional street taco flavors like fresh cilantro and onion.

1 Add the rice and water to the pot and follow the instructions for making brown rice (p. 27).

2 While the rice is cooking, make the marinade by combining all the marinade ingredients in a large bowl. Mix well, then add the steak to the bowl and transfer it to the fridge to marinate for at least 10 minutes.

3 When the rice is done cooking, add ½ cup of the brown rice to each of 8 meal prep containers. Rinse and dry the inner pot and then add the cauliflower florets and 1 cup of water to the pot. Follow the instructions for cooking cauliflower (p. 29).

4 When the cauliflower is done cooking, add 1 cup of the cooked cauliflower to each of the 8 meal prep containers with the rice. Set aside. Rinse and dry the inner pot.

5 When the steak is done marinating, place the trivet in the pot and add the steak and marinade to the pot along with ½ cup of water. Close and lock the lid, then turn the steam release handle to sealing. Select **Pressure Cook (high)** and set the cook time for **5 minutes**. When the cook time is complete, quick release the pressure.

6 Using tongs, transfer the steak to a cutting board, cut into small pieces, and then transfer the steak back to the pot. (Don't be concerned if the steak isn't cooked through at this point.) Select **Sauté** and continue cooking the steak until it's cooked through, about 5 minutes.

7 Use a slotted spoon to divide the steak evenly into the meal prep containers. Top each serving with chopped cilantro and onions. Store in the fridge for up to 4 days or freeze for up to 2 months.

Reheating: Microwave each thawed serving for 2½ to 3 minutes.

Nutrition per serving:
CALORIES: 476; **TOTAL FAT:** 12g; **SATURATED FAT:** 4g; **CHOLESTEROL:** 102g;
SODIUM: 271mg; **TOTAL CARBOHYDRATE:** 46g; **FIBER:** 5g; **PROTEIN:** 43g

TERIYAKI MEATBALL BOWLS

A sweet teriyaki glaze makes these bowls irresistible! Served with whole-grain brown rice and steamed broccoli, these bowls are filling and just might become your favorite meal of the week.

1 Add the rice and water to the pot and follow the instructions for making brown rice (p. 27).

2 While the rice is cooking, combine the ground turkey, eggs, garlic, ginger root, coconut aminos, rolled oats, and green onions in a large bowl, then mix to combine. Spray two egg bite molds with nonstick cooking spray and then fill each cup with the meatball mixture. Cover each mold with aluminum foil.

3 When the rice is done cooking, transfer ⅔-cup servings to each of 7 meal prep containers. Rinse and dry the inner pot, place the trivet in the pot, and add 1 cup of water.

4 Place one egg bite mold on top of the trivet, then place the second egg bite mold on top of the first, making sure to offset the second mold so the cups aren't stacked directly on top of each other. Close and lock the lid, then turn the steam release handle to sealing. Select **Pressure Cook (high)** and set the cook time for **25 minutes**.

5 While the meatballs are cooking, prepare the glaze by combining the ingredients in a medium bowl. Whisk to combine, then set aside.

6 When the cook time for the meatballs is complete, allow the pressure to release naturally, about 10 minutes, then use oven mitts to carefully grasp the trivet handles and remove the molds from the pot. Rinse the inner pot, then add the broccoli and 1 cup of water to the pot and follow the instructions for cooking broccoli (p. 28).

7 While the broccoli is cooking, carefully remove the foil from the molds. One at a time, place a plate upside down on top of each mold and carefully flip the mold and plate so the meatballs fall out onto the plate. Transfer two meatballs to each of the meal prep containers, then drizzle the glaze evenly over the meatballs.

8 When the cook time for the broccoli is complete, divide it equally between the meal prep containers. Store in the fridge for up to 6 days or freeze for up to 2 months.

Reheating: Microwave each thawed serving for 2 to 2½ minutes.

SERVES: 7
SERVING SIZE: 2 MEATBALLS, ⅔ CUP RICE, 1 CUP VEGETABLES

PREP: 20 MINUTES
PRESSURE: 50 MINUTES
TOTAL: 1 HOUR 15 MINUTES

SETTINGS: PRESSURE COOK
RELEASE: NATURAL

2 cups uncooked brown rice

2 cups water

1½lb (680g) ground turkey

2 eggs

1 tbsp minced garlic

1 tsp grated ginger root

1 tsp coconut aminos or reduced-sodium soy sauce

½ cup rolled oats

½ cup chopped green onions (green and white parts)

2 large heads broccoli, cut into small florets (about 7 cups)

FOR THE GLAZE

½ cup diced pineapple

¼ cup coconut aminos or reduced-sodium soy sauce

½ cup water

1 tsp white vinegar

2 tbsp honey

1 tsp minced ginger root

Nutrition per serving:
CALORIES: 470; **TOTAL FAT:** 11g; **SATURATED FAT:** 3g; **CHOLESTEROL:** 72mg; **SODIUM:** 437mg; **TOTAL CARBOHYDRATE:** 68g; **FIBER:** 7g; **PROTEIN:** 28g

SERVES: 4
SERVING SIZE: 1 SCRAMBLE

PREP: 15 MINUTES
PRESSURE: 15 MINUTES
TOTAL: 30 MINUTES

SETTINGS: PRESSURE COOK
RELEASE: QUICK

6 eggs

1 cup plain, unsweetened almond milk

½ cup diced onion (any variety)

½ cup white mushrooms

⅛ tsp salt

⅛ tsp black pepper

¼ cup shredded cheddar cheese

MINI EGG SCRAMBLES

A quick and satisfying breakfast is ready in just a few minutes when you have these savory egg scrambles prepped for the week!

1 Place the trivet in the inner pot and add 1 cup of water. Spray the insides of 4 oven-safe jars, mugs, or ramekins with nonstick cooking spray.

2 Combine the eggs, almond milk, onions, mushrooms, salt, and black pepper in a large bowl. Whisk until the eggs are fully incorporated, then evenly divide the egg mixture into the 4 prepared containers.

3 Sprinkle the cheese over the tops of the containers and then tightly cover each container with aluminum foil. Place the containers on the trivet.

4 Close and lock the lid, then turn the steam release handle to sealing. Select **Pressure Cook (high)** and set the cook time for **15 minutes**. When the cook time is complete, quick release the pressure.

5 Using oven mitts, carefully transfer the egg scrambles to a cooling rack. Carefully remove the foil from the containers and allow the scrambles to cool to room temperature.

6 Once the scrambles have cooled, invert the containers to transfer the scrambles to 4 meal prep containers. (Alternatively, simply re-cover the containers with the foil.) Store in the fridge for up to 4 days. (This recipe does not freeze well.)

Reheating: Microwave servings for 1 to 1½ minutes.

tip *You can substitute ½ cup of any of the following for the onions or mushrooms: finely diced broccoli, finely diced bell peppers, diced green chiles, diced jalapeños, cooked and diced bacon, or ground turkey sausage.*

Nutrition per serving:
CALORIES: 126; **TOTAL FAT:** 8g; **SATURATED FAT:** 2g; **CHOLESTEROL:** 247mg; **SODIUM:** 220mg; **TOTAL CARBOHYDRATE:** 3g; **FIBER:** 1g; **PROTEIN:** 11g

SPICY ENCHILADA CASSEROLE

Diced green chiles give this casserole a spicy bite! This dish tastes like traditional Mexican enchiladas, but it takes much less time to make.

SERVES: 6
SERVING SIZE: 1 CUP

PREP: 5 MINUTES
PRESSURE: 32 MINUTES
TOTAL: 37 MINUTES

SETTINGS: PRESSURE COOK
RELEASE: NATURAL/QUICK

1 Place the trivet in the inner pot and ½ cup of water. Place the chicken breasts on the trivet and top with 2 cans of the diced green chiles. Close and lock the lid, then turn the steam release handle to sealing. Select **Pressure Cook (high)** and set the cook time for **12 minutes**.

2 While the chicken is cooking, cut the tortillas into 4 equal wedges. Set aside.

3 In a large bowl, combine the tomatoes, remaining green chiles, and green chile salsa. Stir then set aside.

4 When the cook time for the chicken is complete, allow the pressure to release naturally for 10 minutes, then quick release the remaining pressure.

5 Transfer the chicken to a large bowl. Use two forks to shred the chicken. (Alternatively, use a hand mixer or stand mixer.) Add the shredded chicken to the bowl with the sauce and then stir to coat.

6 Rinse the inner pot and spray the bottom with nonstick cooking spray. Add the ½ cup of water to the bottom of the pot.

7 Add a layer of the chicken mixture to the bottom of the pot and top with ¾ cup of the cheese, then add a layer of the tortilla pieces. Add the remaining chicken mixture in a second layer, followed by another ¾ cup of cheese and then the remaining tortilla pieces. Top the casserole with the remaining ½ cup of cheese.

8 Close and lock the lid, then turn the steam release handle to sealing. Select **Pressure Cook (low)** and set the cook time for **10 minutes**. When the cook time is complete, quick release the pressure and remove the lid.

9 Divide the casserole into 6 equal-sized servings and transfer them to meal prep containers. Store in the fridge for up to 4 days or freeze for up to 2 months.

Reheating: Microwave each thawed serving for 2½ to 3 minutes.

Ingredients

3lb (1.35kg) boneless, skinless chicken breasts

3 x 4oz (115g) cans diced green chiles, divided

8 corn tortillas

14.5oz (410g) can diced tomatoes

12fl oz (355ml) bottle green chile salsa

½ cup water

2 cups shredded cheddar jack cheese, divided

tip *If you'd like to add some additional spice, replace one can of the diced green chiles in the sauce with one can of diced jalapeños.*

Nutrition per serving:
CALORIES: 412; **TOTAL FAT:** 12g; **SATURATED FAT:** 4g; **CHOLESTEROL:** 102mg; **SODIUM:** 429mg; **TOTAL CARBOHYDRATE:** 31g; **FIBER:** 6g; **PROTEIN:** 42g

WEEK TWO PREP PLAN   63

ORANGE CHICKEN

SERVES: 8
SERVING SIZE: ¾ CUP CHICKEN, ¼ CUP SAUCE, ½ CUP BROWN RICE & ¾ CUP BROCCOLI

PREP: 10 MINUTES
PRESSURE: 7 MINUTES
TOTAL: 32 MINUTES

SETTINGS: SAUTÉ/PRESSURE COOK
RELEASE: NATURAL

2 cups uncooked brown rice

2 cups water

2 large heads broccoli, cut into small florets

½ cup low-sodium chicken broth

½ cup coconut aminos or reduced-sodium soy sauce

½ cup rice vinegar

¼ cup honey

2 tbsp minced fresh ginger root

2 tsp crushed red pepper

4 cloves garlic, minced

Zest and juice of one large orange

3lb (1.35kg) boneless, skinless chicken breasts, cut into 1-inch cubes

1 tbsp arrowroot flour or cornstarch

tip *If you're in a hurry, you can skip thickening the sauce and add this meal right to the prep containers.*

This subtly sweet version of a classic Asian dish is perfectly paired with brown rice and broccoli. It's so easy to prep, cook, and freeze!

1 Spray the inner pot with nonstick cooking spray, add the rice and water to the pot, and follow the instructions for cooking brown rice (p. 27). When the rice is done cooking, divide ½-cup servings into each of 8 meal prep containers.

2 Rinse the inner pot and place the trivet in the pot. Add 1 cup of water and place the broccoli on the trivet, then follow the instructions for cooking broccoli (p. 28). When the broccoli is done cooking, divide ¾-cup servings into the meal prep containers. Rinse the inner pot.

3 Select **Sauté** and lightly spray the inner pot with nonstick cooking spray. Add the chicken broth, coconut aminos, rice vinegar, honey, ginger root, crushed red pepper, garlic, orange zest, and orange juice to the pot.

4 Once the sauce is boiling, add the chicken and stir until the chicken is evenly coated with the sauce.

5 Close and lock the lid, then turn the steam release handle to sealing. Select **Pressure Cook (high)** and set the cook time for **7 minutes**. When the cook time is complete, let the pressure release naturally, about 15 minutes, then remove the lid.

6 Transfer ½ cup of the cooking liquid to a small bowl. Whisk in the arrowroot flour or cornstarch and then add the sauce back to the pot. Select **Sauté** and stir. Allow the chicken to simmer until the sauce thickens, then turn off the pot.

7 Transfer ¾ cup of the chicken and ¼ cup of the sauce to each of the 8 meal prep containers with the rice and broccoli. Store in the fridge for up to 6 days or freeze for up to 2 months.

Reheating: Microwave each thawed serving for 1½ to 2 minutes.

Nutrition per serving:
CALORIES: 465; **TOTAL FAT:** 6g; **SATURATED FAT:** 1g; **CHOLESTEROL:** 109mg; **SODIUM:** 255mg; **TOTAL CARBOHYDRATE:** 58g; **FIBER:** 6g; **PROTEIN:** 44g

EASY LAVA CAKE BITES

Decadent and rich, these subtly sweet cake bites will satisfy your after-dinner sweet cravings. These chocolate and peanut butter treats are one of my family's favorite desserts!

 SERVES: 7
SERVING SIZE: 1 BITE

 PREP: 10 MINUTES
PRESSURE: 5 MINUTES
TOTAL: 15 MINUTES

 SETTINGS: PRESSURE COOK
RELEASE: QUICK

---

4 tsp butter

¼ cup dark chocolate chips plus 14 dark chocolate chips

2 eggs

¼ cup plain, unsweetened almond milk

⅓ cup whole wheat flour

1 tbsp honey

½ tsp baking powder

1 tbsp cocoa powder

⅓ cup peanut butter

1 Spray one egg bite mold with nonstick cooking spray and set aside. Add 1 cup of water to the pot.

2 Combine the butter and ¼ cup of the dark chocolate chips in a large bowl. Microwave the ingredients in 30-second intervals, stirring between each interval, until the ingredients are just melted, then stir well to combine.

3 Add the eggs, almond milk, whole wheat flour, honey, baking powder, and cocoa powder to the bowl. Mix until well combined and smooth.

4 Pour the batter into 7 egg bite cups, filling the cups halfway, then place one chocolate chip in the center of each cup.

5 Divide the peanut butter between the seven cups, adding about 2 teaspoons to each. (Try to place the peanut butter in the center so the batter can surround it.) Place one chocolate chip on top of the peanut butter in each cup, then fill the cups with the remaining batter. Cover the mold with foil.

6 Place the mold on the trivet, then grasp the trivet handles to lower the dish into the pot. Close and lock the lid, then turn the steam release handle to sealing. Select **Pressure Cook (high)** and set the cook time for **5 minutes**. When the cook time is complete, quick release the pressure and then use oven mitts to carefully remove the trivet and egg bite mold from the pot. (If the bottoms of the cake bites aren't finished cooking after 5 minutes, lower the mold back into the pot and place the lid back on the pot to allow the heat to continue cooking the bites for another minute or two.)

7 Using a butter knife, gently loosen each cake bite from the sides of the mold and then set the mold aside to allow the bites to cool for 2–3 minutes. Remove the cooled bites from the mold by placing a plate upside down and on top of the mold, then carefully flip the plate and mold together to allow the cake bites to fall out onto the plate. Store in the fridge for up to 5 days. (These will not freeze well.)

Reheating: Microwave each serving for 30 seconds to 1 minute. (Be careful not to overheat the peanut butter centers.)

tip *For a sweeter cake bite, substitute semi-sweet or milk chocolate chips for the dark chocolate chips.*

If desired, top with a dusting of powdered stevia, fresh fruit, or a dollop of coconut whipped cream.

Nutrition per serving:
CALORIES: 151; **TOTAL FAT:** 11g; **SATURATED FAT:** 5g; **CHOLESTEROL:** 6mg; **SODIUM:** 75mg; **TOTAL CARBOHYDRATE:** 11g; **FIBER:** 2g; **PROTEIN:** 5g

WEEK THREE
PREP PLAN

WEEK THREE PREP PLAN

Meals for the week include a filling Vegetable Frittata, an Asian Chicken Stir-Fry with Ramen, sweet and savory Honey Garlic Chicken Bowls, and a healthier version of a traditional Jambalaya, which features quinoa in place of rice. This prep plan includes double batches of the Jambalaya and Honey Garlic Chicken Bowls.

If desired, you can substitute one or more of the alternate recipes for the primary recipes in a plan. I often will make one of the alternate recipes during a prep day and freeze it in single-serving containers to thaw and reheat later. In order to integrate alternate recipes into your prep plan, reference the meal planning tips on pages 16 and 17 to determine how to swap alternate recipes into your prep session.

PREP PLAN YIELDS

VEGETABLE FRITTATA

×6

ASIAN CHICKEN STIR-FRY WITH RAMEN

×4

RECIPES

PRIMARY

- Vegetable Frittata (p. 72)
- Asian Chicken Stir-Fry with Ramen (p. 75)
- Honey Garlic Chicken Bowls (p. 76)
- Jambalaya with Quinoa (p. 79)

ALTERNATE

- Cheesy Ranch Chicken Casserole (p. 80)
- Sweet Potato Hash with Turkey Sausage (p. 81)
- Classic Lasagna with Ground Turkey (p. 82)
- Banana Bread with Peanut Butter Frosting (p. 83)

HONEY GARLIC CHICKEN BOWLS

×8

JAMBALAYA WITH QUINOA

×16

SHOPPING LIST

PRODUCE

- ○ 1 large piece ginger root
- ○ 5 large heads broccoli
- ○ 8oz (225g) package baby bella mushrooms
- ○ 16oz (455g) package white button mushrooms
- ○ 1 small zucchini
- ○ 1 bell pepper, any color
- ○ 1 small red onion
- ○ 2 large yellow onions
- ○ 1 medium sweet potato
- ○ 2 bunches celery
- ○ 19 cloves garlic
- ○ 1 bunch green onions

MEAT & DAIRY

- ○ 4½lb (2kg) boneless, skinless chicken thighs
- ○ 2½lb (1.15kg) boneless, skinless chicken breasts
- ○ 2½lb (1.15kg) chicken andouille sausage
- ○ 2½lb (1.15kg) raw shrimp
- ○ 9 eggs
- ○ ½ cup plain, unsweetened almond milk
- ○ 1 cup shredded cheddar cheese

PANTRY & DRY GOODS

- ○ ½ cup plus 2 tbsp coconut aminos or low-sodium soy sauce
- ○ 16 tsp olive oil
- ○ 4 brown rice ramen cakes
- ○ 4 cups uncooked white quinoa
- ○ 6 x 15.5oz (440g) cans reduced-sodium diced tomatoes
- ○ 3 tbsp hot sauce
- ○ Nonstick cooking spray

SPICES & SEASONINGS

- ○ 1½ tsp rice vinegar
- ○ 1 tbsp sesame oil
- ○ 1 tsp molasses
- ○ ½ cup plus 3 tbsp honey
- ○ 1⅛ tsp black pepper
- ○ 1 tbsp plus 1 tsp crushed red pepper
- ○ 2 tsp sesame seeds
- ○ ⅛ tsp salt
- ○ 1 tbsp dried thyme
- ○ 1 tbsp dried oregano
- ○ 1 tbsp dried basil
- ○ 4 tsp chili garlic sauce

EQUIPMENT

- ○ 6qt Instant Pot and trivet
- ○ 34 meal prep containers
- ○ 7in round baking pan or oven-safe dish
- ○ Blender or food processor
- ○ Measuring cups
- ○ Measuring spoons
- ○ Large tongs
- ○ Chef's knife
- ○ Cutting board
- ○ Mesh strainer
- ○ Oven mitts
- ○ Large mixing bowls
- ○ 2 large bowls
- ○ Small bowl
- ○ Medium bowl
- ○ 2 one-gallon freezer bags
- ○ Large spoon or spatula
- ○ Slotted spoon

PREP PLAN

(Total Estimated Time: 4½ to 5 hours)

1 Spray a 7-inch oven-safe round baking dish with nonstick cooking spray, set aside. Add 1 cup of water to the inner pot.

2 Dice the vegetables for the **Vegetable Frittata (p. 72),** then follow steps 2–4 to cook the frittata.

3 While the frittata is cooking, chop the broccoli and mushrooms for the **Asian Chicken Stir-Fry (p. 75)** and **Honey Garlic Chicken Bowls (p. 76).** Set 6 cups of broccoli and 2 cups of mushrooms aside in one large bowl for the stir-fry, and set 4 cups of broccoli aside in a medium bowl for the chicken bowls.

4 In a small bowl, follow step 3 to make the sauce for the chicken bowls. Set aside.

5 Dice the onions and celery for two batches of the **Jambalaya with Quinoa (p. 79).**

6 When the frittata is finished cooking, allow the pressure to release naturally, then remove the frittata from the pot and set it aside to cool.

7 Rinse the inner pot and spray with nonstick cooking spray. Make the quinoa for both the jambalaya and chicken bowls by adding 5 cups of water and 4 cups of rinsed quinoa to the pot. Close and lock the lid and then turn the steam release handle to sealing, select **Pressure Cook (high)** and set the cook time for **1 minute.** (Turn off the **Keep Warm** button if your pot has one.)

8 While the quinoa is cooking, follow step 2 to make the sauce for the stir-fry. Pour half of the sauce over the chopped vegetables and set the rest aside.

9 When the quinoa is done cooking, allow the pressure to release naturally for 10 minutes, then divide equal servings into 24 meal prep containers. Wash the inner pot and spray with nonstick cooking spray. Follow step 4 to cook the chicken thighs for the chicken bowls.

10 While the chicken is cooking, divide the cooled frittata into 6 equal servings and transfer them to meal prep containers to complete the recipe.

11 Dice the sausage and chicken for two batches of the jambalaya. Set aside, making sure to keep the raw chicken and sausage separated.

12 When the chicken for the bowls is done cooking, transfer it to a cutting board to cool slightly.

13 Follow steps 5 and 6 to cook the broccoli for the bowls. While the broccoli is cooking, dice the chicken. When the broccoli is done cooking, follow step 7 to complete the recipe.

14 Wash the inner pot and follow steps 3–5 to cook the jambalaya.

15 When the jambalaya is finished cooking, divide equal-sized servings into the 8 remaining containers with quinoa to complete the recipe.

16 Wash the inner pot and spray with nonstick cooking spray. Follow steps 3–6 for the stir-fry. (Make sure to leave the liquid in the pot after completing step 6.)

17 Follow steps 7–8 to finish cooking the ramen for the stir-fry, then divide the mixture between 4 meal prep containers to complete the recipe.

SERVES: 6
SERVING SIZE: 1 SLICE

PREP: 10 MINUTES
PRESSURE: 45 MINUTES
TOTAL: 1 HOUR 5 MINUTES

SETTINGS: PRESSURE COOK
RELEASE: NATURAL

---

9 eggs

½ cup plain, unsweetened almond milk

½ cup diced zucchini

½ cup diced baby bella mushrooms

¼ cup diced bell peppers (any color)

¼ cup diced red onions

½ cup diced broccoli

1 cup finely diced sweet potato

1 cup shredded cheddar cheese

⅛ tsp salt

⅛ tsp black pepper

---

tip *If desired, add ½ cup of diced, cooked bacon or ½ cup of diced, cooked breakfast sausage.*

VEGETABLE FRITTATA

Fresh zucchini, mushrooms, peppers, and broccoli are always in season and pair perfectly with sweet potatoes. This frittata will help keep you feeling full all morning long.

1 Add 1 cup of water to the inner pot and spray a 7-inch round baking pan or oven-safe dish with nonstick cooking spray.

2 In a large bowl, combine the eggs and almond milk. Whisk gently.

3 Add the zucchini, mushrooms, bell peppers, onions, broccoli, sweet potato, cheese, salt, and black pepper to the bowl. Mix gently, then pour the egg mixture into the prepared baking pan and cover with foil. Place the pan on the trivet, then grasp the trivet handles to lower the dish into the pot.

4 Close and lock the lid, then turn the steam release handle to sealing. Select **Pressure Cook (high)** and set the cook time for **45 minutes**. When the cook time is complete, allow the pressure to release naturally for 10 minutes, then quick release any remaining pressure and remove the lid.

5 Use oven mitts to grasp the trivet handles and carefully lift the pan out of the pot. Remove the foil and allow the casserole to cool for 5–10 minutes.

6 Slice the frittata into 6 equal-sized wedges and transfer them to meal prep containers. Store in the fridge for up to 5 days. (This recipe does not freeze well.)

Reheating: Microwave each thawed serving for 1 to 1½ minutes.

Nutrition per serving:
CALORIES: 189; **TOTAL FAT:** 13g; **SATURATED FAT:** 6g; **CHOLESTEROL:** 265mg; **SODIUM:** 294mg; **TOTAL CARBOHYDRATE:** 4g; **FIBER:** 1g; **PROTEIN:** 14g

ASIAN CHICKEN "STIR-FRY" *with Ramen*

A homemade spicy teriyaki sauce creates a unique sweet and spicy flavor in this faux stir-fry. This recipe is packed with vegetables and filling brown rice ramen, and is requested weekly in our home!

SERVES: 4
SERVING SIZE: 2 CUPS

PREP: 15 MINUTES
PRESSURE: 13 MINUTES
TOTAL: 28 MINUTES

SETTINGS: PRESSURE COOK
RELEASE: QUICK

1 Spray the inner pot with nonstick cooking spray.

2 In a blender or food processor, combine the coconut aminos, ginger root, sesame oil, rice vinegar, garlic, black pepper, crushed red pepper (if using), molasses, and honey. Blend until thoroughly combined.

3 Place the chicken thighs in the pot and pour ½ of the sauce over the top, reserving the remaining sauce for later. Add the water to the pot.

4 Close and lock the lid, then turn the steam release handle to sealing. Select **Pressure Cook (high)** and set the cook time for **12 minutes**.

5 While the chicken is cooking, combine the broccoli and mushrooms in a large bowl and then pour the remaining sauce over the vegetables. Set aside.

6 When the cook time for the chicken is complete, quick release the pressure and remove the lid. Transfer the chicken thighs to a large bowl, but do not drain the cooking liquid from the pot. Use two forks to shred the chicken. (Alternatively, use a hand mixer or stand mixer to shred the chicken.) Set aside.

7 Place the ramen cakes in the bottom of the pot and in the cooking liquid, then add the vegetables and sauce. Close and lock the lid, then turn the steam release handle to sealing. Select **Pressure Cook (high)** and set the cook time for **1 minute**. When the cook time is complete, quick release the pressure and remove the lid.

8 Add the chicken back to the pot, then add the sesame seeds, and use tongs to mix the noodles, chicken, and vegetables.

9 Divide 2-cup servings into each of 4 meal prep containers. Store in the fridge for up to 6 days or freeze for up to 1 month.

Reheating: Microwave each thawed serving for 1½ to 2 minutes.

½ cup coconut aminos or reduced-sodium soy sauce

3 tbsp minced ginger root

1 tbsp sesame oil

1½ tsp rice vinegar

1 tsp minced garlic

1 tsp black pepper

1 tsp crushed red pepper (optional)

1 tsp molasses

3 tbsp honey

1½lb (680g) boneless, skinless chicken thighs

¾ cup water

6 cups chopped broccoli

2 cups chopped white button mushrooms

4 brown rice ramen cakes

2 tsp sesame seeds

tip *If preferred, you can substitute store-bought low-sodium teriyaki sauce for the homemade teriyaki sauce.*

If desired, you can substitute whole wheat spaghetti or pad thai noodles for the ramen cakes.

Nutrition per serving:
CALORIES: 385; **TOTAL FAT:** 12g; **SATURATED FAT:** 2g; **CHOLESTEROL:** 162mg; **SODIUM:** 741mg; **TOTAL CARBOHYDRATE:** 32g; **FIBER:** 4g; **PROTEIN:** 38g

SERVES: 4
SERVING SIZE: 1¼ CUPS CHICKEN & BROCCOLI & ½ CUP QUINOA

PREP: 5 MINUTES
PRESSURE: 14 MINUTES
TOTAL: 28 MINUTES

SETTINGS: PRESSURE COOK
RELEASE: QUICK/NATURAL

¾ cup uncooked white quinoa, rinsed

1 cup water

1 tbsp minced garlic

¼ cup honey

2 tbsp coconut aminos or reduced-sodium soy sauce

2 tsp chili garlic sauce or 1 tsp crushed red pepper

1½lb (680g) boneless, skinless chicken thighs

4 cups chopped broccoli florets (about 1 head)

HONEY GARLIC CHICKEN BOWLS

These sweet and savory bowls are delicious meal prep lunches that will last all week in the fridge. They're simple, yet flavorful, chicken bowls that are packed with protein and savory Asian flavors.

1 Spray the inner pot with nonstick cooking spray. Add the rinsed quinoa and 1 cup of water to the inner pot.

2 Close and lock the lid, then turn the steam release handle to sealing. Select **Pressure Cook (high)** and set the cook time for **1 minute**. When the cook time is complete, allow the pressure to release naturally for 10 minutes before quick releasing any remaining pressure. Divide ½-cup servings of the quinoa into 4 meal prep containers. Set aside.

3 In a small bowl, combine the garlic, honey, coconut aminos, and chili garlic sauce. Mix well.

4 Wash the inner pot and spray with nonstick cooking spray. Place the chicken in the pot and pour the sauce over the chicken. Close and lock the lid, then turn the steam release handle to sealing. Select **Pressure Cook (high)** and set the cook time for **12 minutes**. When the cook time is complete, quick release the pressure and remove the lid. Transfer the chicken to a cutting board and dice.

5 Place the trivet in the pot and add the broccoli. (It's okay if some of the pieces fall through to the bottom of the pot.)

6 Close and lock the lid, then turn the steam release handle to sealing. Select **Pressure Cook (high)** and set the cook time for **1 minute**. When the cook time is complete, quick release the pressure and remove the lid. Use oven mitts to remove the trivet from the bottom of the pot, then add the diced chicken and stir.

7 Divide 1¼-cup servings into the meal prep containers containing the quinoa. Store in the fridge for up to 6 days or freeze for up to 2 months.

Reheating: Microwave each thawed serving for 1½ to 2 minutes.

Nutrition per serving:
CALORIES: 422; **TOTAL FAT:** 9g; **SATURATED FAT:** 2g; **CHOLESTEROL:** 162g; **SODIUM:** 330mg; **TOTAL CARBOHYDRATE:** 45g; **FIBER:** 4g; **PROTEIN:** 40g

JAMBALAYA *with Quinoa*

Traditional jambalaya gets a healthier makeover in this version that is packed with creole flavors. This version omits the extra butter and oil and is served over a bed of protein-packed quinoa instead of rice.

 SERVES: 8
SERVING SIZE: 1¾ CUP JAMBALAYA & ½ CUP QUINOA

 PREP: 15 MINUTES
PRESSURE: 6 MINUTES
TOTAL: 33 MINUTES

SETTINGS: PRESSURE COOK
RELEASE: NATURAL/QUICK

1 Spray the inner pot with nonstick cooking spray and then add the rinsed quinoa and water to the pot.

2 Close and lock the lid, then turn the steam release handle to sealing. Select **Pressure Cook (high)** and set the cook time for **1 minute**. When the cook time is complete, allow the pressure to release naturally for 12 minutes, then quick release any remaining pressure. Evenly divide ½-cup servings of the quinoa into 8 meal prep containers and set aside.

3 Rinse the inner pot and place it back in the base. Select **Sauté** and add the olive oil to the pot. When the oil begins to shimmer, add the chicken, onions, celery, and garlic. Sauté for 3–5 minutes or until the ingredients become fragrant and the vegetables begin to soften, then add the sausage, tomatoes, thyme, oregano, basil, crushed red pepper, and hot sauce. Stir to combine.

4 Close and lock the lid, then turn the steam release handle to sealing. Select **Pressure Cook (high)** and set the cook time for **5 minutes**. When the cook time is complete, quick release the pressure, remove the lid, and turn off the pot.

5 Stir in the shrimp, then close the lid to allow the shrimp to cook, about 2 minutes. If the shrimp aren't cooked after 2 minutes, close the lid again and allow them to continue cooking for 3–5 additional minutes.

6 Divide 1¾-cup servings into each of the meal prep containers, then garnish each serving with the chopped green onions. Store in the fridge for up to 6 days or freeze for up to 2 months.

Reheating: Microwave each thawed serving for 1½ to 2 minutes.

1½ cups uncooked white quinoa, rinsed

1¾ cups water

2⅔ tbsp olive oil

1¼lb (565g) boneless, skinless chicken breasts, cut into 1-inch cubes

2 cups chopped yellow onions

1½ cups chopped celery

6 cloves minced garlic

1¼lb (565g) reduced-sodium chicken andouille sausage, diced

3 x 15.5oz (440g) cans reduced-sodium diced tomatoes

1½ tsp dried thyme

1½ tsp dried oregano

1½ tsp dried basil

1½ tsp crushed red pepper

1½ tsp hot sauce

1¼lb (565g) small to medium-sized raw shrimp, peeled, deveined, and tails removed

4 tbsp chopped green onions (green parts only)

tip *To reduce the sodium, omit the chicken sausage and just use chicken and shrimp—the taste is still delicious!*

Nutrition per serving:
CALORIES: 463; **TOTAL FAT:** 19g; **SATURATED FAT:** 3g; **CHOLESTEROL:** 274mg; **SODIUM:** 1377mg; **TOTAL CARBOHYDRATE:** 28g; **FIBER:** 4g; **PROTEIN:** 46g

SERVES: 4
SERVING SIZE: 1¼ CUP

PREP: 10 MINUTES
PRESSURE: 25 MINUTES
TOTAL: 55 MINUTES

SETTINGS: SAUTÉ/PRESSURE COOK
RELEASE: NATURAL

8 slices turkey bacon, diced

1½lb (680g) frozen boneless, skinless chicken breasts

2 tsp minced garlic

1 tsp onion powder

1 tsp dill weed

1 tsp parsley

½ tsp black pepper

1 cup uncooked brown rice

1 cup low-sodium chicken broth

¾ cup plain Greek yogurt

⅔ cup shredded cheddar cheese

CHEESY RANCH CHICKEN CASSEROLE

Savory ranch spices, bacon, and cheesy rice make this a rich and hearty comfort meal. This creamy casserole is delicious warm, or served cold as a vegetable dip.

1 Spray the inner pot with nonstick cooking spray and select **Sauté**. Line a large plate with paper towels.

2 Place the bacon in the pot. Cook for 5 minutes or until the edges begin to curl and the bacon begins to brown, then transfer it to the prepared plate to drain. Set aside.

3 Use a few paper towels to carefully wipe down the inner pot. (It doesn't have to be completely clean, but you'll want to remove any extra grease.)

4 Place the frozen chicken breasts in a single layer in the bottom of the pot. (Do not stack the chicken as it won't cook thoroughly.)

5 Sprinkle the garlic, onion powder, dill weed, parsley, and black pepper over the chicken breasts. Pour the rice over the top of the chicken, then pour the chicken broth over the rice.

6 Close and lock the lid, then turn the steam release handle to sealing. Select **Pressure Cook (high)** and set the cook time for **25 minutes**. When the cook time is complete, allow the pressure to release naturally, then remove the lid.

7 Transfer the chicken breasts to a large bowl and use two forks or a hand mixer to shred the chicken. (If you're using a hand mixer, cut the chicken breasts into two halves first.)

8 Add the shredded chicken back to the pot, then add the Greek yogurt, bacon, and cheddar cheese. Stir to combine.

9 Divide 1¼-cup servings into 4 meal prep containers. Store in the fridge for up to 6 days or freeze for up to 2 months.

Reheating: Microwave each thawed serving for 1½ to 2 minutes.

Nutrition per serving:
CALORIES: 399; **TOTAL FAT:** 17g; **SATURATED FAT:** 7g; **CHOLESTEROL:** 50mg; **SODIUM:** 794mg; **TOTAL CARBOHYDRATE:** 40g; **FIBER:** 2g; **PROTEIN:** 22g

SWEET POTATO HASH
with Turkey Sausage

The cinnamon and nutmeg flavors in this hash pair perfectly with the savory homemade sausage. Homemade turkey sausage is less expensive than the store-bought variety and contains no artificial ingredients.

1 Spray the inner pot with nonstick cooking spray and select **Sauté**.

2 Add the ground turkey, garlic, ¾ cup of the onions, cumin, black pepper, and fennel seed to the pot. Sauté for 12–15 minutes or until the turkey is cooked through and no pink remains.

3 Add the sweet potatoes, the remaining ¾ cup of the onions, cinnamon, nutmeg, and water to the pot.

4 Close and lock the lid, then turn the steam release handle to sealing. Select **Pressure Cook (high)** and set the cook time for **5 minutes**. When the cook time is complete, quick release the pressure, remove the lid, and gently stir.

5 Divide ¾-cup servings into 8 meal prep containers. Store in the fridge for up to 6 days or freeze for up to 2 months.

Reheating: Microwave each thawed serving for 1½ to 2 minutes.

 SERVES: 8
SERVING SIZE: ¾ CUP

PREP: 20 MINUTES
PRESSURE: 5 MINUTES
TOTAL: 35 MINUTES

 SETTINGS: SAUTÉ/PRESSURE COOK
RELEASE: QUICK

2lbs (905g) ground turkey

2 tbsp minced garlic

1½ cups diced red onions, divided

2 tsp cumin

1 tsp black pepper

2 tsp fennel seed

6 cups peeled and diced sweet potatoes, cut into ½-inch cubes

1 tbsp ground cinnamon

1 tsp ground nutmeg

1 cup water

tip *If desired, you can add scrambled eggs to this dish. Remove the cooked hash from the pot, spray the inner pot with nonstick cooking spray, and select **Sauté**. Add the eggs and scramble until cooked, about 3–5 minutes, then combine with the hash.*

Nutrition per serving:
CALORIES: 269; **TOTAL FAT:** 10g; **SATURATED FAT:** 2g; **CHOLESTEROL:** 84mg; **SODIUM:** 134mg; **TOTAL CARBOHYDRATE:** 23g; **FIBER:** 3g; **PROTEIN:** 23g

SERVES: 6
SERVING SIZE: 1 SLICE

PREP: 15 MINUTES
PRESSURE: 25 MINUTES
TOTAL: 1 HOUR

SETTINGS: SAUTÉ/PRESSURE COOK
RELEASE: NATURAL

1lb (450g) ground turkey

28oz (795g) can crushed tomatoes

1 tbsp dried oregano

1 tbsp dried thyme

1 tbsp dried parsley

1 tsp black pepper

1 tbsp onion powder

1 tbsp minced garlic

12oz (340g) box whole-grain lasagna noodles

1 cup part-skim ricotta

¾ cup shredded mozzarella plus ¼ cup for topping

tip *If desired, replace the crushed tomatoes and seasonings with one 25oz (705g) jar of store-bought pasta sauce.*

CLASSIC LASAGNA
with Ground Turkey

This turkey lasagna uses a simple homemade sauce and whole-grain noodles to reduce the preservatives and also keep you feeling full. Italian seasonings help make this recipe taste like an old family favorite.

1 Spray a 7-inch round baking pan or oven-safe dish with nonstick cooking spray. Set aside.

2 Spray the bottom of the inner pot with nonstick cooking spray and select **Sauté**. Once the pot is hot, add the ground turkey and sauté for 7–10 minutes or until thoroughly cooked, then use a slotted spoon to transfer the turkey to a plate. Set the turkey aside and turn off the pot.

3 In a medium bowl, make the sauce by combining the crushed tomatoes, oregano, thyme, parsley, black pepper, onion powder, and garlic. Stir until well combined. (Note: Avoid using canned diced tomatoes, which can make the lasagna watery.)

4 Add a thin layer of the sauce to the bottom of the prepared baking pan. Next, add a layer of noodles (breaking them into pieces to fit if necessary), then add a layer of ricotta cheese, followed by a layer of mozzarella cheese and then a layer of ground turkey. Repeat the process until all of the ingredients have been added to the pan, then top the lasagna with the remaining ¼ cup of mozzarella cheese. Cover the dish with foil. Place the dish on the trivet, grasp the trivet handles, and carefully lower the dish into the pot.

5 Add 2 cups of water to the pot. Close and lock the lid, then turn the steam release handle to sealing. Select **Pressure Cook (high)** and set the cook time for **25 minutes**. When the cook time is complete, allow the pressure to release naturally, then remove the lid and use oven mitts to carefully remove the lasagna from the pot.

6 Cut the lasagna into 6 equal servings and place them in meal prep containers. Store in the fridge for up to 6 days or freeze for up to 2 months.

Reheating: Microwave each thawed serving for 1 to 1½ minutes.

Nutrition per serving:
CALORIES: 452; **TOTAL FAT:** 14g; **SATURATED FAT:** 6g; **CHOLESTEROL:** 80mg; **SODIUM:** 370mg; **TOTAL CARBOHYDRATE:** 55g; **FIBER:** 3g; **PROTEIN:** 32g

BANANA BREAD
with Peanut Butter Frosting

Whole wheat flour and a simple, low-sugar frosting make this sweet treat perfect for anyone who is craving a healthier, lower-sugar option to traditional banana bread.

1   Place the trivet in the inner pot and add 2 cups of water. Spray a 7-inch round baking pan or oven-safe dish with nonstick cooking spray. Set aside.

2   Add the bananas to a medium bowl and mash them with a fork, then add the eggs, maple syrup, almond milk, vanilla extract, whole wheat flour, baking powder, baking soda, and salt. Mix until the eggs and ingredients are well combined.

3   Add the mixture to the prepared pan and tightly cover with aluminum foil. Place the pan on the trivet and grasp the handles to carefully lower it into the pot.

4   Close and lock the lid, then turn the steam release handle to sealing. Select **Pressure Cook (high)** and set the cook time for **35 minutes**.

5   While the bread is cooking, make the frosting by combining the peanut butter and maple syrup in a small bowl. Set aside.

6   When the cook time for the bread is complete, let the pressure release naturally, about 15 minutes, then use oven mitts to carefully grasp the trivet handles and remove the dish from the pot.

7   Carefully remove the foil from the dish and let the bread cool to room temperature. Once the bread has cooled, use a spatula to spread the peanut butter frosting over the top of the bread.

8   Cut the bread into 8 equal slices and transfer them to meal prep containers. Store in the fridge for up to 6 days. (This recipe does not freeze well.)

Reheating: Microwave individual servings for 15 seconds.

SERVES: 8
SERVING SIZE: 1 SLICE

PREP: 15 MINUTES
PRESSURE: 35 MINUTES
TOTAL: 90 MINUTES

SETTINGS: PRESSURE COOK
RELEASE: NATURAL

FOR THE BREAD

2 large, ripe bananas

2 eggs

⅔ cup maple syrup

⅓ cup unsweetened plain or vanilla almond milk

1½ tsp vanilla extract

1⅓ cup whole wheat flour

1 tsp baking powder

½ tsp baking soda

¼ tsp salt

FOR THE FROSTING

⅓ cup creamy peanut butter

2 tbsp maple syrup

tip *If you prefer to eat this bread warm, it's best to store the frosting in a separate container and spread it over the bread after reheating.*

Nutrition per serving:
CALORIES: 184; **TOTAL FAT:** 2g; **SATURATED FAT:** 1g; **CHOLESTEROL:** 41mg; **SODIUM:** 105mg; **TOTAL CARBOHYDRATE:** 39g; **FIBER:** 3g; **PROTEIN:** 4g

WEEK FOUR PREP PLAN

WEEK FOUR PREP PLAN

Meals for the week include four recipes that focus on my favorite—vegetables! This plan features a flavorful Breakfast Ratatouille, a filling Vegetarian Chili, a super-simple Chicken and Rice with Broccoli and Mushrooms, and a Loaded Vegetable Goulash. Note that for this plan, you'll be making two batches of the Breakfast Ratatouille.

If desired, you can substitute one or more of the alternate recipes for the primary recipes in a plan. I often will make one of the alternate recipes during a prep day and freeze it in single-serving containers to thaw and reheat later. In order to integrate alternate recipes into your prep plan, reference the meal planning tips on pages 16 and 17 to determine how to swap alternate recipes into your prep session.

PREP PLAN YIELDS

BREAKFAST RATATOUILLE

×12

CHICKEN & RICE WITH BROCCOLI & MUSHROOMS

×8

RECItPES

PRIMARY

- Breakfast Ratatouille (p. 90)
- Chicken and Rice with Broccoli and Mushrooms (p. 93)
- Loaded Vegetable Goulash (p. 94)
- Vegetarian Chili (p. 97)

ALTERNATE

- Turkey Chorizo and Egg Breakfast Burritos (p. 98)
- Spaghetti with Turkey Meatballs (p. 99)
- Tuscan Chicken Pasta (p. 100)
- Lightened-Up Lemon Bars (p. 101)

LOADED VEGETABLE GOULASH

×6

VEGETARIAN CHILI

×8

BREAKFAST RATATOUILLE

SERVES: 6
SERVING SIZE: 1¼ CUPS

PREP: 15 MINUTES
PRESSURE: 40 MINUTES
TOTAL: 55 MINUTES

SETTINGS: PRESSURE COOK
RELEASE: QUICK

1 medium red onion,
cut into ½-inch slices

2 medium zucchini,
cut into ½-inch slices

3 medium yellow squash,
cut into ½-inch slices

2 medium Roma tomatoes,
cut into ½-inch slices

1 tsp minced garlic

½ cup chopped fresh parsley

¼ tsp salt

¼ tsp black pepper

1 tsp dried thyme

1 tsp dried basil

6 eggs

⅓ cup plain, unsweetened
almond milk

1 small red bell pepper,
seeded and chopped

Savory Italian flavors are paired with fresh squash, tomatoes, and onions in this hearty breakfast dish. The addition of eggs makes this traditional ratatouille recipe perfect for breakfast!

1 Spray a 7-inch round baking pan or oven-safe dish with nonstick cooking spray. Add 1½ cups of water to the bottom of the inner pot.

2 In a large bowl, combine the onions, zucchini, squash, and tomatoes.

3 In a small bowl, combine the garlic, parsley, salt, black pepper, thyme, and basil. Add half of the seasoning mixture to the bowl with the sliced vegetables, then toss to coat. Reserve the remaining seasoning for later.

4 In a medium bowl, combine the eggs, almond milk, and diced bell peppers. Stir to combine.

5 Place a single layer of the sliced vegetables in the bottom of the prepared baking pan. Continue adding layers of the vegetables until the dish is full. (Don't worry if each layer isn't completely full—the egg mixture will fill it in.)

6 Pour the egg mixture on top of the vegetables, then sprinkle the remaining seasoning mixture over the top. Cover the dish with aluminum foil, place the dish on the trivet, then grasp the trivet handles to lower the dish into the pot.

7 Close and lock the lid, then turn the steam release handle to sealing. Select **Pressure Cook (high)** and set the cook time for **40 minutes.** When the cook time is complete, quick release the pressure, remove the lid, and use oven mitts to carefully grasp the trivet handles and remove the dish from the pot. Set aside to cool for 10 minutes.

8 Slice the ratatouille into 6 equal servings (about 1¼ cup each) and transfer the servings to meal prep containers. Store in the fridge for up to 6 days or freeze for up to 2 months.

Reheating: Microwave each thawed serving for 1 to 1½ minutes.

Nutrition per serving:
CALORIES: 110; **TOTAL FAT:** 5g; **SATURATED FAT:** 1g; **CHOLESTEROL:** 164mg; **SODIUM:** 187mg; **TOTAL CARBOHYDRATE:** 10g; **FIBER:** 3g; **PROTEIN:** 8g

CHICKEN AND RICE
with Broccoli and Mushrooms

This easy recipe is filling, nutritious, and satisfying! The simple flavors of rosemary and oregano are all that are needed for this hearty meal.

SERVES: 8
SERVING SIZE: 1½ CUPS

PREP: 5 MINUTES
PRESSURE: 20 MINUTES
TOTAL: 35 MINUTES

SETTINGS: PRESSURE COOK
RELEASE: NATURAL/QUICK

1 Spray the inner pot with nonstick cooking spray. Add the rice and chicken broth to the pot.

2 Place the frozen chicken thighs on top of the rice, then add the rosemary, oregano, salt, and black pepper.

3 Close and lock the lid, then turn the steam release handle to sealing. Select **Pressure Cook (high)** and set the cook time for **20 minutes.** When the cook time is complete, allow the pressure to release naturally for 10 minutes, then quick release the remaining pressure and remove the lid.

4 Transfer the chicken to a large bowl and then close the lid to keep the heat in the pot. Use two forks to shred the chicken, then return the shredded chicken to the pot.

5 Add the broccoli and mushrooms on top of the chicken and rice. Close the lid to allow the remaining heat in the pot to cook the broccoli for 10 minutes, then remove the lid and use a large spoon to stir the ingredients.

6 Divide 1½-cup servings into 8 meal prep containers. Store in the fridge for up to 6 days or freeze for up to 2 months.

Reheating: Microwave each thawed serving for 1½ to 2 minutes.

2 cups uncooked brown rice

1½ cups low-sodium chicken broth

1½lb (680g) frozen boneless, skinless chicken thighs

2 tsp dried rosemary

2 tsp dried oregano

⅛ tsp salt

⅛ tsp black pepper

4 cups chopped broccoli (about 2 heads)

2 cups diced baby bella mushrooms

Nutrition per serving:
CALORIES: 295; **TOTAL FAT:** 4g; **SATURATED FAT:** 1g; **CHOLESTEROL:** 54mg; **SODIUM:** 166mg; **TOTAL CARBOHYDRATE:** 41g; **FIBER:** 3g; **PROTEIN:** 24g

SERVES: 6
SERVING SIZE: 1¼ CUPS

PREP: 15 MINUTES
PRESSURE: 3 MINUTES
TOTAL: 21 MINUTES

SETTINGS: SAUTÉ/PRESSURE COOK
RELEASE: QUICK

1lb (453g) lean ground turkey

2 tbsp minced garlic

2½ tbsp Italian seasoning

1 small onion (white or yellow), minced

2 bay leaves

1 cup chopped zucchini

1 cup chopped bell peppers (any color)

1 cup whole wheat elbow macaroni

14oz (395g) can crushed tomatoes

14fl oz (415ml) water

LOADED VEGETABLE GOULASH

Also called "chop suey" in American cuisine, this healthier version of a traditional dish is made with whole-grain pasta and packed with vegetables. It's both filling and nutritious!

1 Select **Sauté** and lightly spray the inner pot with nonstick cooking spray.

2 Once the pot is hot, add the ground turkey and use a spatula to break the meat into crumbles. Sauté for 7–10 minutes or until the meat is browned, then add the garlic, Italian seasoning, onions, bay leaves, zucchini, and bell peppers. Sauté for 1 additional minute or until the vegetables begin to soften.

3 Add the macaroni to the pot and then top the pasta with the crushed tomatoes. Fill the tomato can with water and pour the water into the pot.

4 Close and lock the lid, then turn the steam release handle to sealing. Select **Pressure Cook (high)** and set cook time for **3 minutes.** When the cook time is complete, quick release the pressure and remove the lid. Discard the bay leaves and stir.

5 Divide 1¼-cup servings into 6 meal prep containers. Store in the fridge for up to 6 days or freeze for up to 2 months.

Reheating: Microwave each thawed serving for 1½ to 2 minutes.

tip *If desired, you can substitute a 24oz (680g) jar of meat-free pasta sauce for the garlic, Italian seasoning, bay leaves, and crushed tomatoes.*

Nutrition per serving:
CALORIES: 238; **TOTAL FAT:** 7g; **SATURATED FAT:** 2g; **CHOLESTEROL:** 56g; **SODIUM:** 145mg; **TOTAL CARBOHYDRATE:** 27g; **FIBER:** 2g; **PROTEIN:** 20g

VEGETARIAN CHILI

This vegetarian chili features a base of fresh vegetables, filling beans, and hearty brown rice for a delicious meatless meal. If you prefer to include meat, you can easily add it. (See instructions in tip.)

SERVES: 8
SERVING SIZE: 1 CUP

PREP: 10 MINUTES
PRESSURE: 24 MINUTES
TOTAL: 44 MINUTES

SETTINGS: PRESSURE COOK
RELEASE: QUICK

1   Spray the inner pot with nonstick cooking spray. Add the rice and water to the pot and then follow the steps for making brown rice (p. 27).

2   When the cooking time for the rice is complete, allow the pressure to release naturally for 10 minutes, then quick release the remaining pressure. Transfer the rice to a medium bowl and set aside.

3   Rinse the inner pot and add the bell peppers, onions, black beans, cannellini beans, kidney beans, chili powder, cumin, garlic powder, onion powder, salt, black pepper, diced tomatoes, and vegetable broth to the pot. Stir well.

4   Close and lock the lid, then turn the steam release handle to sealing. Select **Pressure Cook (high)** and set the cook time for **4 minutes.** When the cook time is complete, quick release the pressure and remove the lid. Add the cooked rice back to the pot and stir well to combine the ingredients.

5   Divide 1-cup servings into 8 meal prep containers. Store in the fridge for up to 6 days or freeze for up to 2 months.

Reheating: Microwave each thawed serving for 1½ to 2 minutes.

1 cup uncooked brown rice

1 cup water

1½ cups diced bell peppers, any color

1½ cups diced red onion

15oz (425g) can black beans, drained

15oz (425g) can cannellini beans, drained

15oz (425g) can kidney beans, drained

1½ tbsp chili powder

1½ tbsp cumin

1½ tsp garlic powder

½ tsp onion powder

1 tsp salt

¼ tsp black pepper

15oz (425g) can diced tomatoes

3 cups low-sodium vegetable broth

tip *If you'd like to add ground meat to this recipe, sauté one pound of ground turkey or ground beef in the pot before adding the other ingredients. (If using ground beef, drain before adding other ingredients.)*

Nutrition per serving:
CALORIES: 209; **TOTAL FAT:** 1g; **SATURATED FAT:** 1g; **CHOLESTEROL:** 0mg; **SODIUM:** 577mg; **TOTAL CARBOHYDRATE:** 41g; **FIBER:** 9g; **PROTEIN:** 10g

SERVES: 8
SERVING SIZE: 1 BURRITO

PREP: 5 MINUTES
PRESSURE: 20 MINUTES
TOTAL: 25 MINUTES

SETTINGS: SAUTÉ
RELEASE: NONE

2lb (905g) ground turkey

1 tsp onion powder

1 tsp garlic powder

4 tbsp chili powder

1 tbsp cumin

1 tbsp ground coriander

1 tbsp dried oregano

1 tsp black pepper

2 tsp paprika

¼ tsp ground cinnamon

1 tsp crushed red pepper

1 tbsp fennel seed

2 tbsp apple cider vinegar

1 medium bell pepper (any color), seeded and chopped

1 medium zucchini, chopped

8 eggs

8 large whole wheat flour tortillas

½ cup shredded cheddar cheese

tip *If preferred, you can store the cheese, chorizo mixture, and tortillas separately in the fridge and assemble the burritos when you're ready to eat.*

TURKEY CHORIZO AND EGG BREAKFAST BURRITOS

Mexican chorizo and eggs is a traditional breakfast in the Southwest, but it's often made with pork sausage. This healthier version is made with ground turkey, but it still features traditional chorizo seasonings.

1   Lightly spray the inner pot with nonstick cooking spray and select **Sauté (medium).**

2   Combine the ground turkey, onion powder, garlic powder, chili powder, cumin, coriander, oregano, black pepper, paprika, cinnamon, red pepper, fennel, apple cider vinegar, bell peppers, and zucchini in a large bowl. Mix well.

3   Add the turkey mixture to the pot, using a spatula to break apart any large chunks. Sauté, stirring frequently, for 7–10 minutes or until the temperature of the turkey reaches 165°F (74°C) and no pink color remains. (Note: Because of the color of the seasonings in this recipe, it might be difficult to see the color of the meat, so it's always best to use a thermometer to check the temperature.)

4   Use a spoon to push the cooked chorizo to one side of the pot. Spray the other side with nonstick cooking spray and crack the eggs into the pot. Scramble the eggs and then stir to combine them with the chorizo.

5   Add a ¾-cup portion of the filling to the center of one tortilla, top with 1 tablespoon of the shredded cheddar cheese, then roll into a burrito. Repeat with the remaining ingredients, then transfer the burritos to 8 meal prep containers. Store in the fridge for up to 6 days. (This recipe does not freeze well.)

Reheating: Microwave each serving for 1½ to 2 minutes.

Nutrition per serving:
CALORIES: 303; **TOTAL FAT:** 13g; **SATURATED FAT:** 4g; **CHOLESTEROL:** 207mg; **SODIUM:** 434mg; **TOTAL CARBOHYDRATE:** 25g; **FIBER:** 4g; **PROTEIN:** 22g

SPAGHETTI
with Turkey Meatballs

Spaghetti and meatballs has never been easier! Classic Italian flavors shine in these meatballs, and the ground turkey and whole-grain pasta make this a healthier version of a family favorite.

1 In a medium bowl, combine the ground turkey, black pepper, Italian seasoning, onion powder, and garlic powder. Mix well to combine, then use your hands to form 24 equal-sized meatballs.

2 Add the olive oil to the bottom of the inner pot and select **Sauté (medium)**.

3 When the oil begins to shimmer, place six of the meatballs in the pot and brown for about 1 minute per side. Transfer the browned meatballs to a plate and repeat with the remaining meatballs.

4 Once all of the meatballs are browned, add ¼ cup of the chicken broth to the pot, then use a spatula to gently deglaze the bottom of the pot.

5 Place the meatballs back in the pot, then break the noodles in half and spread them evenly over the top of the meatballs. Add the bay leaves, spaghetti sauce, and remaining chicken broth, but do not stir.

6 Close and lock the lid, then turn the steam release handle to sealing. Select **Pressure Cook (high)** and set the cook time for **4 minutes**. When the cook time is complete, quick release the pressure and remove the lid. Discard the bay leaves, then stir until the pasta and sauce are well combined.

7 Divide ¾-cup servings of the pasta and sauce into 8 meal prep containers, then top each serving with 3 meatballs. Store in the fridge for up to 6 days or freeze for up to 2 months.

Reheating: Microwave each thawed serving for 2 to 2½ minutes, stirring halfway through the reheating time.

SERVES: 8
SERVING SIZE: 3 MEATBALLS & ¾ CUP OF SPAGHETTI AND SAUCE

PREP: 25 MINUTES
PRESSURE: 4 MINUTES
TOTAL: 29 MINUTES

SETTINGS: SAUTÉ/PRESSURE COOK
RELEASE: QUICK

2lb (905g) ground turkey

½ tsp black pepper

1 tbsp Italian seasoning

1 tsp onion powder

1 tsp garlic powder

1 tbsp extra virgin olive oil

2 cups low-sodium chicken broth, divided

16oz (455g) box whole wheat spaghetti

2 bay leaves

24oz (680g) jar no-sugar-added spaghetti sauce

tip *If you prefer to use homemade sauce, omit the jarred spaghetti sauce and use the crushed tomatoes and spices from the Classic Lasagna with Ground Turkey recipe (p. 81).*

Nutrition per serving:
CALORIES: 413; **TOTAL FAT:** 13g; **SATURATED FAT:** 3g; **CHOLESTEROL:** 84mg; **SODIUM:** 546mg; **TOTAL CARBOHYDRATE:** 48g; **FIBER:** 1g; **PROTEIN:** 32g

SERVES: 6
SERVING SIZE: 1⅓ CUPS

PREP: 15 MINUTES
PRESSURE: 3 MINUTES
TOTAL: 20 MINUTES

SETTINGS: PRESSURE COOK
RELEASE: QUICK

1 cup halved grape tomatoes

3 cloves garlic, minced

1 tbsp Italian seasoning

¼ tsp black pepper

2lb (905g) boneless, skinless chicken breasts, cut into 1-inch cubes

12oz (340g) whole wheat penne

2½ cups low-sodium chicken broth

¾ cup plain 2% Greek yogurt

¾ cup 2% cottage cheese

2 cups baby leaf spinach

¼ cup fresh basil leaves

⅔ cup grated Parmesan cheese

tip *If desired, substitute oil-free sun-dried tomatoes for the grape tomatoes.*

TUSCAN CHICKEN PASTA

This creamy whole-grain pasta dish is filling and packed with protein. It's a healthier spin on a comfort-food dish that features traditional Italian seasonings but with lighter ingredients.

1 Lightly spray the inner pot with nonstick cooking spray. Select **Sauté.**

2 Add the grape tomato halves, garlic, Italian seasoning, and black pepper to the pot. Sauté for 2–3 minutes or until the seasonings become fragrant, then add the chicken and stir. Continue sautéing for 7–10 additional minutes or until the chicken is evenly browned, then add the penne on top of the chicken and pour the chicken broth over the top, but do not stir.

3 Close and lock the lid, then turn the steam release handle to sealing. Select **Pressure Cook (high)** and set the cook time for **3 minutes**.

4 While the pasta is cooking, combine the Greek yogurt and cottage cheese in a blender or food processor. Blend until smooth, then set aside.

5 When the cook time for the chicken is complete, quick release the pressure and remove the lid. Add the spinach and basil to the pot and stir until the leaves have wilted, then carefully remove the inner pot and drain off any excess liquid.

6 Return the inner pot to the base. Add the Parmesan cheese along with the yogurt and cottage cheese mixture. Stir to combine.

7 Divide 1⅓-cup servings into 6 meal prep containers. Store in the fridge for up to 6 days or freeze for up to 2 months.

Reheating: Microwave each thawed serving for 1½ to 2 minutes.

Nutrition per serving:
CALORIES: 472; **TOTAL FAT:** 10g; **SATURATED FAT:** 4g; **CHOLESTEROL:** 107mg; **SODIUM:** 519mg; **TOTAL CARBOHYDRATE:** 41g; **FIBER:** 5g; **PROTEIN:** 52g

LIGHTENED-UP LEMON BARS

These flavorful bars are the perfect combination of tart and sweet. Using honey as a sweetener removes the refined sugar from this lighter version of a classic dessert.

SERVES: 16
SERVING SIZE: 1 BAR

PREP: 10 MINUTES
PRESSURE: 20 MINUTES
TOTAL: 2 HOURS 40 MINUTES

SETTINGS: PRESSURE COOK
RELEASE: NATURAL

1 Add 2 cups of water to the inner pot. Spray a 7-inch round baking pan or oven-safe dish with nonstick cooking spray. Set aside.

2 Begin making the crust by combining the coconut flour, eggs, coconut oil, and honey in a small bowl. Mix until a dough forms. Transfer the dough to the prepared pan and spread it evenly across the bottom of the pan, then use the bottom of a glass to firmly press the dough into the bottom. Transfer the crust to the freezer to set for 10 minutes.

3 While the crust is setting, make the filling by combining the honey, eggs, coconut flour, salt, and lemon juice in a small bowl. Whisk until the filling forms a smooth, consistent texture.

4 Remove the crust from the freezer and pour the filling over the chilled dough. Cover the dish tightly with aluminum foil, place the dish on the trivet, and grasp the handles to carefully lower it into the pot.

5 Close and lock the lid, then turn the steam release handle to sealing. Select **Pressure Cook (high)** and set the cook time for **20 minutes**. When the cook time is complete, let the pressure release naturally, then remove the lid and use oven mitts to carefully grasp the trivet handles and remove the dish from the pot.

6 Place the bars in the refrigerator to set for two hours, then cut them into 16 equal-sized pieces. Store in an airtight container in the fridge for up to 6 days. (These do not freeze well.)

FOR THE CRUST
¾ cup coconut flour

2 eggs

⅓ cup coconut oil

1 tbsp honey

FOR THE FILLING
½ cup honey

2 eggs

1 tbsp coconut flour

¼ tsp salt

¼ cup freshly squeezed lemon juice (about 2 large lemons)

tip *For lime bars, replace the lemon juice with an equal amount of freshly squeezed lime juice.*

Nutrition per serving:
CALORIES: 118; **TOTAL FAT:** 6g; **SATURATED FAT:** 5g; **CHOLESTEROL:** 41mg; **SODIUM:** 65mg; **TOTAL CARBOHYDRATE:** 14g; **FIBER:** 2g; **PROTEIN:** 2g

WEEK FIVE
PREP PLAN

WEEK FIVE PREP PLAN

Meals for this week include Sweet & Savory Breakfast Potatoes, Kung Pao Chicken with lots of vegetables, a hearty Spicy White Chicken Chili, and a comforting Stuffed Pepper Soup. These flavorful recipes are some of my personal favorites! Note that you will be making a double batch of the Kung Pao Chicken.

If desired, you can substitute one or more of the alternate recipes for the primary recipes in a plan. I often will make one of the alternate recipes during a prep day and freeze it in single-serving containers to thaw and reheat later. In order to integrate alternate recipes into your prep plan, reference the meal planning tips on pages 16 and 17 to determine how to swap alternate recipes into your prep session.

PREP PLAN YIELDS

SWEET & SAVORY BREAKFAST SWEET POTATOES

×8

KUNG PAO CHICKEN

×12

RECINES

SPICY WHITE CHICKEN CHILI

×8

STUFFED PEPPER SOUP

×4

SHOPPING LIST

PRODUCE

- ○ 1 small red onion
- ○ 3 medium yellow onions
- ○ 2 medium orange or yellow bell peppers
- ○ 4 medium red bell peppers
- ○ 4 medium green bell peppers
- ○ 21 cloves garlic
- ○ 6 poblano peppers
- ○ 4 jalapeño peppers
- ○ 2 tbsp ginger root (about 2 small pieces)
- ○ 4 heads broccoli
- ○ 1 small bunch cilantro
- ○ 4 small sweet potatoes
- ○ 2 large bananas

MEAT & DAIRY

- ○ 1lb (455g) extra lean ground turkey
- ○ 8lb (3.60kg) boneless, skinless chicken breasts
- ○ 1½ cups 2% plain Greek yogurt
- ○ 4 eggs

PANTRY & DRY GOODS

- ○ 14.5oz (410g) can diced tomatoes
- ○ 15oz (425g) can tomato sauce
- ○ 6 cups low-sodium chicken broth
- ○ 2 cups dry white beans
- ○ 3½ cups uncooked brown rice
- ○ 1⅓ cup coconut aminos or reduced-sodium soy sauce
- ○ 8 tbsp honey
- ○ 8 tbsp peanut butter
- ○ ½ tsp plain rice vinegar
- ○ 1 tsp sesame oil
- ○ 1 tsp sriracha sauce
- ○ 2 tbsp cornstarch
- ○ 1 cup unsalted peanuts
- ○ 2¼ cups plain, unsweetened almond milk
- ○ Nonstick cooking spray

SPICES & SEASONINGS

- ○ 2 tsp dried oregano
- ○ 1 tbsp cumin
- ○ 1 tbsp chili powder
- ○ 1⅓ tsp black pepper
- ○ ¼ tsp salt

EQUIPMENT

- ○ 6qt Instant Pot and trivet
- ○ 32 meal prep containers
- ○ Measuring cups
- ○ Measuring spoons
- ○ Chef's knife
- ○ Cutting board
- ○ Small bowl
- ○ Medium bowl
- ○ Wooden spoon
- ○ Spatula
- ○ Whisk
- ○ Strainer

PREP PLAN

(Total Estimated Time: 3 to 3½ hours)

1 Spray the inner pot with nonstick cooking spray. Add 3 cups of dry brown rice and 3 cups of water to the pot and follow the instructions for cooking brown rice (p. 27).

2 While the rice is cooking, prepare the vegetables and follow step 2 to make the sauce for two batches of the **Kung Pao Chicken (p. 111)**. (Note that you'll be doubling this recipe, but you'll be cooking each batch separately.)

3 When the brown rice is finished cooking, equally divide it between 12 meal prep containers and set them aside.

4 Rinse the inner pot and follow steps 3-7 to make the first batch of the kung pao chicken. (Place the chicken for the second batch in the refrigerator until you're ready to cook it.)

5 While the chicken is cooking, begin prepping the vegetables for the **Stuffed Pepper Soup (p. 115).**

6 When the first batch of kung pao chicken is finished cooking, divide it into the 6 meal prep containers containing the brown rice and then follow steps 3-7 to cook the second batch.

7 While the second batch of chicken is cooking, finish prepping the vegetables and measure out the spices for the stuffed pepper soup.

8 When the second batch of Kung Pao Chicken is finished cooking, separate it into the 6 meal prep containers with the brown rice to complete the recipe.

9 Wash the inner pot and follow steps 1-4 to cook the stuffed pepper soup.

10 While the soup is cooking, wash and poke holes in the sweet potatoes for the **Sweet & Savory Breakfast Sweet Potatoes (p. 108).**

11 When the stuffed pepper soup is finished cooking, divide the soup into 4 meal prep containers to complete the recipe.

12 Wash the inner pot. Add 1 cup of water and place the trivet in the pot. Add the sweet potatoes to the pot and follow step 3 to cook the potatoes.

13 While the sweet potatoes are cooking, slice the bananas and then follow step 4 to prepare the egg mixture for the savory potatoes.

14 When the sweet potatoes are done cooking, cut them in half lengthwise and transfer them to 8 meal prep containers.

15 Follow steps 5 and 6 to prepare the savory toppings for the potatoes. When the preparation for the toppings is complete, follow step 7 to complete the recipe.

16 Wash the inner pot and follow steps 1-5 to make the **Spicy White Chicken Chili (p. 112)**. When the chili is finished cooking, divide it among the remaining meal prep containers to complete the recipe.

SERVES: 8
SERVING SIZE: ½ POTATO PLUS TOPPINGS

PREP: 15 MINUTES
PRESSURE: 16 MINUTES
TOTAL: 41 MINUTES

SETTINGS: PRESSURE COOK/SAUTÉ
RELEASE: NATURAL

4 small sweet potatoes

4 tbsp peanut butter

2 cups sliced bananas

4 eggs

¼ cup plain, unsweetened almond milk

⅛ tsp salt

⅛ tsp black pepper

1 cup diced red bell peppers

⅓ cup diced yellow onions

PEANUT BUTTER BANANA SWEET POTATOES
Nutrition per serving:
CALORIES: 217
TOTAL FAT: 8g
SATURATED FAT: 2g
CHOLESTEROL: 0mg
SODIUM: 110mg
TOTAL CARBOHYDRATE: 10g
FIBER: 3g
PROTEIN: 8g

SOUTHWEST SCRAMBLED EGG SWEET POTATOES
Nutrition per serving:
CALORIES: 138
TOTAL FAT: 5g
SATURATED FAT: 1g
CHOLESTEROL: 164mg
SODIUM: 121mg
TOTAL CARBOHYDRATE: 17g
FIBER: 5g
PROTEIN: 7g

Sweet & Savory BREAKFAST SWEET POTATOES

Filling, slow-burning carbs like the ones in these potatoes are the perfect way to start your day. There are two versions of this recipe below—sweet and savory—so you can choose your favorite or mix and match!

1. Place the trivet in the inner pot and add 1 cup of water.

2. Use a fork or the tip of a sharp knife to poke holes over the entire surface of the potatoes, then place them on top of the trivet.

3. Close and lock the lid, then turn the steam release handle to sealing. Select **Pressure Cook (high)** and set the cook time for **16 minutes.** When the cook time is complete, allow the pressure to release naturally and then remove the lid. Cut the potatoes in half lengthwise and place them in 8 meal prep containers.

4. Combine the eggs, almond milk, salt, and black pepper in a medium bowl, then whisk to combine. Set aside.

5. Rinse the inner pot and spray it with nonstick cooking spray. Select **Sauté** and add the bell peppers and onions to the pot. Sauté 1–2 minutes, stirring frequently with a spatula, until the vegetables have softened

6. Pour the egg mixture into the pot and use the spatula to stir until the eggs are scrambled, about 5 minutes.

7. Top each of four of the potato halves with 1 tablespoon of the peanut butter and ½ cup of the sliced bananas. Top each of the remaining four potato halves with ¼ of the scrambled egg mixture. Store in the fridge for up to 4 days. (This recipe does not freeze well.)

Reheating: Microwave each serving for 1 to 1½ minutes.

KUNG PAO CHICKEN

A sweet and savory homemade hoisin sauce will make this vegetable-packed recipe a family favorite! This filling recipe is satisfying and topped with cilantro and crunchy peanuts for an authentic flavor.

SERVES: 6
SERVING SIZE: 1½ CUPS

PREP: 10 MINUTES
PRESSURE: 30 MINUTES
TOTAL: 55 MINUTES

SETTINGS: PRESSURE COOK/SAUTÉ
RELEASE: QUICK

1 Add the rice and water to the pot and then follow the instructions for cooking brown rice (p. 27). When the rice is done cooking, transfer equal portions to 6 meal prep containers. Set aside.

2 In a small bowl, combine the coconut aminos, honey, ginger root, peanut butter, rice vinegar, sesame oil, garlic, and sriracha sauce. Whisk to combine.

3 Rinse the inner pot then spray with nonstick cooking spray. Add the diced chicken and sauce to the pot, then stir to coat the chicken pieces in the sauce.

4 Close and lock the lid, then turn the steam release handle to sealing. Select **Pressure Cook (high)** and set the cook time for **10 minutes**. When the cook time is complete, quick release the pressure and remove the lid.

5 Select **Sauté** and use a spoon to move the chicken to one side of the pot. Add the cornstarch to the opposite side and use a whisk or fork to mix the cornstarch into the sauce. (Do not combine the chicken with the sauce.)

6 Once the sauce begins to bubble, cook for 1–2 minutes while continuously stirring, then turn off the pot and mix the chicken in with the sauce. Add the diced peppers and broccoli.

7 Close and lock the lid, then turn the steam release handle to sealing. Select **Pressure Cook (high)** and set the cook time for **0 (zero) minutes.** When the cook time is complete, quick release the pressure and remove the lid.

8 Mix the vegetables in with the chicken and divide 1½-cup portions into the 6 meal prep containers. Garnish each serving with equal amounts of the cilantro and peanuts. Store in the fridge for up to 6 days or freeze for up to 2 months.

Reheating: Microwave each thawed serving for 1 to 1½ minutes.

1½ cups uncooked brown rice

1½ cups water

⅔ cup coconut aminos or reduced-sodium soy sauce

¼ cup honey

1 tbsp freshly grated ginger root

2 tbsp peanut butter

¼ tsp plain rice vinegar

½ tsp sesame oil

2 tbsp minced garlic

½ tsp sriracha sauce

3lb (1.35kg) boneless, skinless chicken breasts, diced

1 tbsp cornstarch

1 medium red bell pepper, seeded and chopped

1 medium green bell pepper, seeded and chopped

4 cups finely chopped broccoli

¼ cup chopped cilantro, to garnish

½ cup unsalted peanuts, to garnish

Nutrition per serving:
CALORIES: 649; **TOTAL FAT:** 17g; **SATURATED FAT:** 3g; **CHOLESTEROL:** 145mg; **SODIUM:** 802mg; **TOTAL CARBOHYDRATE:** 65g; **FIBER:** 5g; **PROTEIN:** 58g

SERVES: 8
SERVING SIZE: 2 CUPS

PREP: 10 MINUTES
PRESSURE: 45 MINUTES
TOTAL: 1 HOUR 10 MINUTES

SETTINGS: PRESSURE COOK
RELEASE: QUICK/NATURAL

---

2 cups dry white beans (not soaked)

6 small poblano peppers, diced

4 small jalapeño peppers, diced

2 medium bell peppers (any color), seeded and diced

2 medium yellow onions, diced

8 cloves garlic, minced

1 tbsp cumin

1 tbsp chili powder

1 tsp black pepper

4 cups low-sodium chicken broth

2 cups plain, unsweetened almond milk

2lb (905g) frozen boneless, skinless chicken breasts

1½ cups plain 2% Greek yogurt

tip *If you prefer this dish be less spicy, omit the jalapeño and poblano peppers.*

To make this dairy-free, omit the Greek yogurt.

SPICY WHITE CHICKEN CHILI

One of my favorite ways to cook in the Instant Pot is combining frozen chicken and dry beans—the cook times match up perfectly and it makes for an easy dump-and-go meal. The bold southwest flavors in this chili make this recipe a monthly staple in our home.

1 Lightly spray the inner pot with nonstick cooking spray.

2 Add the white beans, poblano peppers, jalapeño peppers, bell peppers, onions, garlic, cumin, chili powder, black pepper, chicken broth, and almond milk to the pot. Stir, then place the frozen chicken breasts on top of the mixture.

3 Close and lock the lid, then turn the steam release handle to sealing. Select **Pressure Cook (high)** and set cook time for **45 minutes.** When the cook time is complete, allow the pressure to release naturally for 10 minutes, then quick release the remaining pressure and remove the lid.

4 Transfer the chicken to a large bowl and use two forks to shred. (Alternatively, use a hand mixer or stand mixer to shred the chicken.)

5 Stir the Greek yogurt into the bean mixture and then add the shredded chicken back to the pot. Stir again.

6 Scoop 2-cup servings into 8 meal prep containers. Store in the fridge for up to 6 days or freeze for up to 2 months.

Reheating: Microwave each thawed serving for 2 to 2½ minutes.

Nutrition per serving:
CALORIES: 296; **TOTAL FAT:** 6g; **SATURATED FAT:** 1g; **CHOLESTEROL:** 75g;
SODIUM: 274mg; **TOTAL CARBOHYDRATE:** 25g; **FIBER:** 6g; **PROTEIN:** 37g

STUFFED PEPPER SOUP

This simple recipe is perfect for meal prep because it keeps well in the fridge, and can be frozen and thawed while still retaining its hearty texture. Whole-grain rice and a full serving of vegetables help make this recipe both filling and healthy!

SERVES: 4
SERVING SIZE: 2 CUPS

PREP: 10 MINUTES
PRESSURE: 8 MINUTES
TOTAL: 26 MINUTES

SETTINGS: SAUTÉ/PRESSURE COOK
RELEASE: QUICK

1 Select **Sauté** and spray the inner pot with nonstick cooking spray. Add the ground turkey to the pot and use a spatula to break apart any large pieces. Sauté the turkey, stirring frequently, for 7–10 minutes or until browned.

2 Add the onions, bell peppers, diced tomatoes, tomato sauce, chicken broth, brown rice, garlic, oregano, and black pepper. Stir to combine.

3 Close and lock the lid, then turn the steam release handle to sealing. Select **Pressure Cook (high)** and set the cook time for **8 minutes**. When the cook time is complete, quick release the pressure and remove the lid.

4 Add salt to taste, then divide 2-cup servings into each of 4 meal prep containers. Store in the fridge for up to 6 days or freeze for up to 2 months.

Reheating: Microwave each thawed serving for 1½ to 2 minutes.

1lb (455g) lean ground turkey

1 small red onion, chopped

3 small bell peppers (2 green and 1 red), seeded and chopped

14.5oz (410g) can diced tomatoes

15oz (425g) can tomato sauce

2 cups chicken broth

½ cup uncooked brown rice

1 clove garlic, minced

2 tsp dried oregano

¼ tsp black pepper

Salt to taste

Nutrition per serving:
CALORIES: 358; **TOTAL FAT:** 11g; **SATURATED FAT:** 3g; **CHOLESTEROL:** 84mg; **SODIUM:** 687mg; **TOTAL CARBOHYDRATE:** 38g; **FIBER:** 6g; **PROTEIN:** 29g

SERVES: 6
SERVING SIZE: ⅔ CUP MEAT & 2
LETTUCE SHELLS

 PREP: 10 MINUTES
PRESSURE: 12 MINUTES
TOTAL: 35 MINUTES

 SETTINGS: PRESSURE COOK/SAUTÉ
RELEASE: QUICK

2lb (905g) boneless, skinless
chicken breasts

3 tsp minced garlic

¾ cup coconut aminos or reduced-
sodium soy sauce

¼ cup peanut butter

2 tbsp honey

1 tbsp plain rice vinegar

1⅔ tbsp toasted sesame oil

2 tsp minced ginger root

1 tbsp sriracha sauce

½ cup diced red onion

2 cups diced baby Portobello
mushrooms

4oz (115g) can water chestnuts,
drained and chopped

3 green onions (green and white
parts), chopped

2 heads romaine or butter lettuce,
cut into shells (discard the
outermost and innermost
portions)

---

tip *You can also use ground
chicken or turkey for this recipe.
Eliminate steps 1 and 2 and
simply sauté the meat for 5–7
minutes before adding the
vegetables and sauce.*

CHICKEN LETTUCE WRAPS

Juicy chicken, healthy vegetables, and a homemade hoisin sauce come together for this light, but filling, dish. This healthier version of the restaurant favorite is an easy meal prep recipe!

1 Place the chicken in the pot and add 1 cup of water.

2 Close and lock the lid and flip the steam release handle to sealing. Select **Pressure Cook (high)** and set the cook time for **12 minutes**.

3 While the chicken is cooking, make the sauce by combining the garlic, coconut aminos, peanut butter, honey, rice vinegar, sesame oil, ginger root, and sriracha sauce in a medium bowl. Use a fork to whisk the ingredients until well combined.

4 When the cook time for the chicken is complete, transfer the chicken to a large bowl and use two forks to shred. (Alternatively, use a stand mixer or hand mixer to shred the chicken.)

5 Rinse and dry the inner pot and spray with nonstick cooking spray. Select **Sauté** and add ¼ of the sauce to the pot along with the onions, mushrooms, and water chestnuts. Sauté for 2–3 minutes or until the onions become soft.

6 Add the chicken back to the pot and then pour the remaining sauce over the top of the chicken. Stir until the chicken and vegetables are evenly coated in the sauce. Continue sautéing for 5 additional minutes.

7 Divide ⅔-cup servings into 6 meal prep containers, sprinkle the green onions over each serving, then add 2 lettuce shells to each container. Store in the fridge for up to 6 days or freeze (chicken mixture only) for up to 2 months. Do not freeze the lettuce shells.

Reheating: Microwave each thawed serving of the chicken mixture for 1 to 1½ minutes.

Nutrition per serving:
CALORIES: 381; **TOTAL FAT:** 14g; **SATURATED FAT:** 3g; **CHOLESTEROL:** 97mg;
SODIUM: 845mg; **TOTAL CARBOHYDRATE:** 26g; **FIBER:** 6g; **PROTEIN:** 39g

APPLE OAT CRUMBLE

This delicious treat will satisfy any sweet tooth! I've made this classic crumble recipe a bit healthier by using honey and almond flour. The honey helps bring out the natural sweetness of the apples.

1 Select **Sauté** and preheat the pot for 1 minute, then spray the inner pot with nonstick cooking spray and turn off the pot.

2 Add the water, apples, nutmeg, honey, and 1 teaspoon of the cinnamon. Close and lock the lid, then turn the steam release handle to sealing. Select **Pressure Cook (high)** and set the cook time for **2 minutes**.

3 While the apples are cooking, combine the oats, almond flour, brown sugar, butter, and remaining cinnamon in a small bowl. Use a spoon to combine. (If the butter is too hard to mix with a spoon, use your hands to combine the ingredients.)

4 When the cook time for the apples is complete, quick release the pressure and remove the lid. Using oven mitts, carefully remove the inner pot from the base and drain any extra liquid from the pot, then sprinkle the oat topping evenly over the top of the apples.

5 Preheat the oven to broil. Place the inner pot in the oven and broil for 1 minute, then remove the pot from the oven and place it back in the base to cool for 5–10 minutes.

6 Once the crumble is cooled, divide 1-cup portions into 6 meal prep containers. Store in the fridge for up to 4 days or freeze for up to 2 months.

Reheating: Enjoy cold, or warm thawed portions in the microwave for 45 seconds to 1 minute.

SERVES: 6
SERVING SIZE: 1 CUP

PREP: 15 MINUTES
PRESSURE: 2 MINUTES
TOTAL: 18 MINUTES

SETTINGS: SAUTÉ/PRESSURE COOK
RELEASE: QUICK

¼ cup water

6 medium apples, cored and diced (preferably Honeycrisp or Pink Lady varieties)

¼ tsp ground nutmeg

2 tbsp honey

2 tsp ground cinnamon, divided

1 cup uncooked rolled oats

½ cup almond flour

¼ cup light brown sugar

2 tbsp butter, softened

tip *If you have an air fryer lid for your Instant Pot, you can air fry the top of the crumble instead of broiling it.*

Nutrition per serving:
CALORIES: 194; **TOTAL FAT:** 9g; **SATURATED FAT:** 3g; **CHOLESTEROL:** 10mg; **SODIUM:** 4mg; **TOTAL CARBOHYDRATE:** 26g; **FIBER:** 2g; **PROTEIN:** 4g

WEEK SIX
PREP PLAN

WEEK SIX PREP PLAN

Meals for this week include a perfectly sweet French Toast Casserole, protein-packed Spaghetti Squash Lasagna Boats, Beef Gyros with Tzatziki Sauce, and one of our family favorites—Garlic Pork with Mashed Sweet Potatoes and Broccoli. Note that you'll be making two batches of the Spaghetti Squash Lasagna Boats for this week's plan.

If desired, you can substitute one or more of the alternate recipes for the primary recipes in a plan. I often will make one of the alternate recipes during a prep day and freeze it in single-serving containers to thaw and reheat later. In order to integrate alternate recipes into your prep plan, reference the meal planning tips on pages 16 and 17 to determine how to swap alternate recipes into your prep session.

PREP PLAN YIELDS

FRENCH TOAST CASSEROLE

×8

SPAGHETTI SQUASH LASAGNA BOATS

×4

RECIPES

BEEF GYROS WITH TZATZIKI SAUCE

×8

GARLIC PORK WITH MASHED SWEET POTATOES & BROCCOLI

×6

SHOPPING LIST

PRODUCE

- ○ 2 small spaghetti squash
- ○ 1 large head cauliflower
- ○ 1 cup baby leaf spinach
- ○ 1 medium red onion
- ○ 14 cloves garlic
- ○ 1 small lemon
- ○ 1 medium cucumber
- ○ 1 English cucumber
- ○ Fresh dill
- ○ 1 small head lettuce
- ○ 2 small tomatoes
- ○ 2lb (905g) sweet potatoes (about 3 medium)
- ○ 2 heads broccoli

MEAT & DAIRY

- ○ 2lb (905g) flank steak
- ○ 3lb (1.35kg) pork tenderloin
- ○ 4 eggs
- ○ 2½ cups plain, unsweetened almond milk
- ○ 1½ cups plain 2% Greek yogurt
- ○ ½ cup 2% cottage cheese
- ○ ½ cup shredded mozzarella
- ○ ½ cup feta cheese
- ○ 2 tbsp butter

PANTRY & DRY GOODS

- ○ ½ cup plus 2 tbsp coconut aminos or reduced-sodium soy sauce
- ○ 16 tsp olive oil
- ○ 4 brown rice ramen cakes
- ○ 4 cups uncooked white quinoa
- ○ 6 x 15.5oz (440g) cans reduced-sodium diced tomatoes
- ○ 3 tbsp hot sauce
- ○ Nonstick cooking spray

SPICES & SEASONINGS

- ○ 20oz (565g) loaf whole wheat bread (preferably stale)
- ○ 4 pita bread pockets
- ○ ¼ cup maple syrup
- ○ ½ cup no-sugar-added pasta sauce
- ○ ½ cup low-sodium beef broth
- ○ 1 tsp apple cider vinegar
- ○ 1⅓ tbsp olive oil
- ○ 1 cup low-sodium chicken broth
- ○ 2 tbsp cornstarch

EQUIPMENT

- ○ 6qt Instant Pot and trivet
- ○ 26 meal prep containers
- ○ 2 egg bite molds
- ○ 7in round baking pan or oven-safe dish
- ○ Vegetable peeler
- ○ Chef's knife
- ○ Fork
- ○ Spoon
- ○ Wooden spoon
- ○ Spatula
- ○ Cutting board
- ○ Strainer
- ○ Small bowl
- ○ 3 medium bowls
- ○ Aluminum foil
- ○ Plastic wrap
- ○ Small resealable plastic bags
- ○ Food processor or potato masher
- ○ Large baking sheet

PREP PLAN

(Total Estimated Time: 3 to 3½ hours)

1 Follow steps 1–6 to make the **French Toast Casserole (p. 126)**.

2 While the French toast casserole is cooking, follow step 1 to prepare the spices for the **Garlic Pork with Mashed Sweet Potatoes and Broccoli (p. 133)**. Rub the spices into the pork pieces and set aside.

3 Peel and dice the sweet potatoes into 1-inch chunks and make the foil bowl to cook them in (step 3), then transfer the potatoes to the foil bowl. Rinse and cut the broccoli into small florets. Set aside.

4 Prep the squash and other ingredients for the **Spaghetti Squash Lasagna Boats (p. 129)**. Halve both squash lengthwise and scrape out the seeds with a spoon. Follow step 3 to make two batches of the squash boat filling, then transfer the filling to the refrigerator until it's time to make the boats.

5 Prepare the lettuce, tomatoes, onions, and cucumbers for the **Beef Gyros with Tzatziki Sauce (p. 130)**. Follow step 2 to season the flank steak, then jump to step 5 to prepare the tzatziki sauce. Cover the sauce with plastic wrap and transfer to the fridge until ready to use.

6 When the cook time for the casserole is complete, cut it into 8 equal-sized servings and transfer to meal prep containers to complete the recipe.

7 Rinse the inner pot. Add 2 cups of water and place the trivet in the pot. Follow steps 1 and 2 to cook the squash and cauliflower by placing two spaghetti squash halves on the trivet and then adding half of the cauliflower to the pot.

8 While the squash and cauliflower are cooking, remove the squash boat filling from the fridge and gather the ingredients to assemble the boats. Once the spaghetti squash and cauliflower are finished cooking, remove them from the pot and set aside to cool. Repeat steps 1 and 2 to cook the remaining squash halves and cauliflower.

9 While the second batch of squash and cauliflower is cooking, follow steps 4–6 and use half of the squash boat filling to prepare the first batch of squash boats.

10 When the second batch of squash and cauliflower is finished cooking, set it aside to cool briefly, then repeat steps 4–6 to prepare the second batch of squash boats with the remaining filling.

11 Preheat the oven to broil. Place the prepared squash boats on a large baking sheet and broil for 1–2 minutes or until the cheese is brown and bubbly, then remove them from the oven and transfer to 4 meal prep containers to complete the recipe.

12 Rinse the inner pot and follow steps 2 and 4 to cook the garlic pork and potatoes. When the cook time for the pork and potatoes is complete, continue following step 4 to cook the broccoli.

13 While the broccoli is cooking, follow step 5 to make the mashed sweet potatoes.

14 When the cook time for the broccoli is complete, remove the broccoli and pork from the pot. Follow steps 6 and 7 to make the gravy and slice the pork. Transfer the pork, gravy, mashed sweet potatoes, and broccoli to 6 meal prep containers to complete the recipe.

15 Wash the inner pot and follow steps 1, 3, 4, 6, and 7 to cook the steak for the gyros. When the cook time for the steak is complete, follow steps 7 and 8 to complete the recipe.

SERVES: 8
SERVING SIZE: 1 SLICE

PREP: 15 MINUTES
PRESSURE: 1 HOUR 5 MINUTES
TOTAL: 1 HOUR 30 MINUTES

SETTINGS: PRESSURE COOK
RELEASE: NATURAL/QUICK

20oz (565g) loaf whole-grain bread (preferably stale), torn into small chunks

4 eggs

2 cups plain, unsweetened almond milk

2 tbsp ground cinnamon

2 tsp ground nutmeg

2 tbsp vanilla extract

2 tbsp coconut sugar

¼ cup maple syrup

tip *This recipe can also be made into French Toast Cups using egg bite molds. Pack three molds with the mixture, then cover the molds with foil. Cook two molds on high pressure for 30 minutes with a natural release, then remove the molds from the pot and cook the third mold for 20 minutes with a natural release. (Serving size is 3 cups.)*

FRENCH TOAST CASSEROLE

Cinnamon and sugar combine to make this breakfast recipe a delicious sweet treat, while whole-grain bread, almond milk, and coconut sugar make it healthier.

1 Preheat the oven on the lowest setting to 200°F (95°C). Place the trivet in the inner pot and add 1½ cups of water. Coat a 7-inch round baking pan or oven-safe dish with nonstick cooking spray and set aside.

2 Scatter the bread chunks in a single layer across a large baking sheet. Place in the oven for 15–20 minutes or until the bread becomes dry and crusty. (Note: If the bread is already stale and sufficiently dry, this step can be skipped.)

3 Add the eggs to a large bowl and use a fork to whisk, then add the almond milk, cinnamon, nutmeg, vanilla extract, coconut sugar, and maple syrup. Continue whisking until well combined.

4 Add the bread pieces to the bowl and use a large spoon to mix until the bread is coated evenly in the egg mixture.

5 Transfer the bread mixture to the prepared baking pan, lightly pressing the bread chunks down into the pan so they're well packed. Cover the pan with foil and place it on the trivet, then grasp the trivet handles to lower the dish into the pot.

6 Close and lock the lid, then turn the steam release handle to sealing. Select **Pressure Cook (high)** and set the cook time for **65 minutes**. When the cook time is complete, allow the pressure to release naturally for 10 minutes, then quick release the remaining pressure and remove the lid.

7 Use oven mitts to grasp the trivet handles and carefully lift the pan out of the pot. Remove the foil and allow the casserole to cool for 5 minutes before cutting it into 8 equal-sized servings and placing in meal prep containers. Store in the fridge for up to 6 days or freeze for up to 2 months.

Reheating: Microwave each thawed serving for 30 seconds to 1 minute.

Nutrition per serving:
CALORIES: 253; **TOTAL FAT:** 5g; **SATURATED FAT:** 1g; **CHOLESTEROL:** 82mg; **SODIUM:** 403mg; **TOTAL CARBOHYDRATE:** 39g; **FIBER:** 5g; **PROTEIN:** 12g

SPAGHETTI SQUASH LASAGNA BOATS

These boats are protein-packed and filling! They have all the flavors of traditional lasagna, with a bounty of veggies and extra protein from the addition of the cottage cheese and Greek yogurt.

SERVES: 2
SERVING SIZE: 1 BOAT

PREP: 10 MINUTES
PRESSURE: 7 MINUTES
TOTAL: 32 MINUTES

SETTINGS: PRESSURE COOK
RELEASE: NATURAL

1 small spaghetti squash, halved and seeded

1½ cups chopped cauliflower

¼ cup 2% cottage cheese

¼ cup plain 2% Greek yogurt

1½ tsp minced garlic

1 tsp dried basil

1 tsp dried oregano

½ tsp dried parsley

¼ cup no-sugar-added pasta sauce

½ cup baby leaf spinach

¼ cup shredded mozzarella

1 Place the trivet in the inner pot and add 2 cups of water.

2 Place both halves of the spaghetti squash flat on the trivet. (If they don't sit flat, lean them against the sides of the pot.) Add the cauliflower on top of the spaghetti squash. Close and lock the lid, then flip the steam release handle to sealing. Select **Pressure Cook (high)** and set the cook time for **7 minutes**.

3 While the squash is cooking, combine the cottage cheese, Greek yogurt, garlic, basil, oregano, and parsley in a blender or food processor. Process on high for 30 seconds or until smooth and creamy, then transfer the mixture to a medium bowl.

4 When the cook time for the squash is complete, allow the pressure to release naturally—about 10 minutes—then remove the lid. Transfer the cauliflower to the bowl with the cottage cheese mixture and use a fork to mash it into the other ingredients. Preheat the broiler on high.

5 Using a fork, hollow out each squash half, but do not discard the shells (If the squash doesn't easily scrape out, place the shells back in the pot and pressure cook for 3 more minutes with a natural release.) Add the squash to the bowl with the cauliflower and cottage cheese mixture, then stir until well combined.

6 Spoon one half of the squash mixture into each of the squash shells, then top each with 1 tablespoon of the pasta sauce, a layer of the spinach, and 2 tablespoons of the mozzarella. Place the boats on a large baking sheet and broil for 1–2 minutes or until the cheese is melted and golden brown.

7 Transfer the boats to 2 meal prep containers. Store in the fridge for up to 6 days or freeze for up to 2 months.

Reheating: Microwave each thawed serving for 1½ to 2 minutes.

tip *The cook time for the squash can differ slightly, depending on the size and age of the squash, so adjust as needed.*

Nutrition per serving:
CALORIES: 255; **TOTAL FAT:** 7g; **SATURATED FAT:** 3g; **CHOLESTEROL:** 13mg; **SODIUM:** 482mg; **TOTAL CARBOHYDRATE:** 41g; **FIBER:** 9g; **PROTEIN:** 14g;

SERVES: 8
SERVING SIZE: ¾ CUP MEAT, 2 TBSP
TZATZIKI SAUCE & ½ PITA BREAD

PREP: 20 MINUTES
PRESSURE: 7 MINUTES
TOTAL: 27 MINUTES

SETTINGS: SAUTÉ/PRESSURE COOK
RELEASE: NATURAL/QUICK

BEEF GYROS
with Tzatziki Sauce

A homemade creamy dill tzatziki sauce is the star of this recipe. Savory parsley, onion, and garlic combine for an authentic taste that's also healthier than a traditional gyro!

FOR THE GYROS

1 tsp olive oil

2lb (905g) flank steak

1 tbsp dried parsley

1 tsp black pepper

1 medium red onion, sliced

3 cloves garlic, minced

½ cup low-sodium beef broth

1 tbsp lemon juice

1 tsp apple cider vinegar

1 cup shredded lettuce

1 cup chopped tomatoes

1 cup chopped cucumber

½ cup feta cheese

4 whole wheat pita breads, cut into halves

FOR THE TZATZIKI SAUCE

1 cup plain 2% Greek yogurt

½ English cucumber, peeled, seeded, and finely chopped

1 clove garlic, minced

2 tbsp chopped fresh dill

1 Select **Sauté** and add the olive oil to the pot.

2 Season both sides of the flank steak with the parsley and black pepper, then slice the steak against the grain and into thin strips.

3 Add the onions, garlic, and steak strips to the pot. Sauté for 1–2 minutes or until the garlic and onions are fragrant and the meat begins to brown. Add the beef broth, lemon juice, and apple cider vinegar, then use a wooden spoon to scrape any browned bits from the bottom of the pot.

4 Close and lock the lid, then turn the steam release handle to sealing. Select **Pressure Cook (high)** and set the cook time for **7 minutes**.

5 While the steak is cooking, make the tzatziki sauce by combining the Greek yogurt, English cucumber, garlic, and dill in a small bowl. Cover with plastic wrap and transfer to the refrigerator.

6 When the cook time for the meat is complete, allow the pressure to release naturally for 10 minutes, then quick release the remaining pressure and remove the lid. Use a spoon to transfer the steak to a medium bowl to cool.

7 While the meat is cooling, equally divide the lettuce, tomatoes, and cucumber between 8 meal prep containers, placing the vegetables to one side of each container, then equally dividing the feta cheese over the vegetables. Scoop ¾-cup servings of the meat into the empty side of each container. Place the pitas in plastic bags or wrap in plastic wrap.

8 When ready to serve, add the vegetables to one pita half and then reheat the meat in the microwave. Add the warm meat to the pita and top with 2 tablespoons of the tzatziki sauce. Store the meat and sauce in the fridge for up to 6 days. (The meat can be frozen for up to 2 months.)

Reheating: Microwave each thawed serving of the meat for 30 seconds to 1 minute.

Nutrition per serving:
CALORIES: 290; **TOTAL FAT:** 9g; **SATURATED FAT:** 4g; **CHOLESTEROL:** 78g;
SODIUM: 329mg; **TOTAL CARBOHYDRATE:** 20g; **FIBER:** 3g; **PROTEIN:** 32g

GARLIC PORK *with Mashed Sweet Potatoes and Broccoli*

Perfectly cooked pork tenderloin with fresh garlic is paired with mashed sweet potatoes, steamed broccoli, and a quick gravy in this hearty meal.

1 In a small bowl, combine the garlic, basil, parsley, oregano, salt, and black pepper. Use a fork to mix, then rub the seasonings into the tops of the pork pieces.

2 Select **Sauté** and add the olive oil to the inner pot. When the oil begins to shimmer, place the pork pieces, seasoned sides down, in the pot. Sauté for 1 minute, flip the pieces and sauté the bottoms for 1 more minute, then transfer the pieces to a plate and turn off the pot. Add the chicken broth and use a spatula to deglaze the pot, then stir. Place the trivet in the pot and place the pork pieces on top of the trivet.

3 Make a foil bowl for the sweet potatoes by placing a 14-inch piece of aluminum foil on a flat surface and spraying it with nonstick cooking spray. Place the cubed sweet potatoes on the foil and slowly roll the sides in to make a bowl. Place the bowl directly on top of the pork.

4 Close and lock the lid, then turn the steam release handle to sealing. Select **Pressure Cook (high)** and set the cook time for **10 minutes**. When the cook time is complete, allow the pressure to release naturally for 5 minutes, then quick release the remaining pressure and remove the lid. Using oven mitts, carefully transfer the potatoes to a large bowl. Add the broccoli to the pot and on top of the pork. Close and lock the lid again, then turn the steam release handle to sealing. Select **Pressure Cook (high)** and set the cook time for **1 minute**.

5 While the broccoli is cooking, add the butter to the bowl with the sweet potatoes. Use a potato masher to mash the potatoes while slowly adding the almond milk until a creamy consistency is achieved.

6 When the broccoli is done cooking, quick release the pressure, transfer the broccoli and pork to a plate, and remove the trivet. Select **Sauté**. Add the cornstarch and whisk vigorously. Once the gravy thickens, turn off the pot and use oven mitts to remove the inner pot from the base.

7 Slice the pork and equally divide it into 6 meal prep containers. Top with equal amounts of the gravy, then add equal amounts of the sweet potatoes and broccoli to each container. Store in the fridge for up to 6 days or freeze for up to 2 months.

Reheating: Microwave each thawed serving for 1½ to 2 minutes.

SERVES: 6
SERVING SIZE: ½LB PORK, ½ CUP MASHED SWEET POTATOES & 1 CUP BROCCOLI

PREP: 10 MINUTES
PRESSURE: 11 MINUTES
TOTAL: 30 MINUTES

SETTINGS: SAUTÉ/PRESSURE COOK
RELEASE: QUICK

¼ cup minced garlic (about 8 cloves)

2 tbsp dried basil

2 tsp dried parsley

2 tsp dried oregano

¼ tsp salt

¼ tsp black pepper

3lb (1.35kg) pork tenderloin, cut into two pieces

1 tbsp olive oil

1 cup low-sodium chicken broth

2lb (905g) sweet potatoes (about 3 medium), peeled and cut into 1-inch chunks

2 heads broccoli, cut into small florets

2 tbsp butter

½ cup plain, unsweetened almond milk

2 tbsp cornstarch

Nutrition per serving:
CALORIES: 520; **TOTAL FAT:** 12g; **SATURATED FAT:** 5g; **CHOLESTEROL:** 158mg; **SODIUM:** 310mg; **TOTAL CARBOHYDRATE:** 47g; **FIBER:** 10g; **PROTEIN:** 57g

SERVES: 4
SERVING SIZE: ½ CUP

 PREP: 5 MINUTES
PRESSURE: 5 MINUTES
TOTAL: 10 MINUTES

 SETTINGS: PRESSURE COOK
RELEASE: NATURAL/QUICK

---

1 cup uncooked steel-cut oats

1½ cups plain, unsweetened almond milk

1 tbsp light brown sugar

1 tbsp honey

STEEL-CUT OATS
with Brown Sugar and Honey

These super-simple oats are subtly sweet, perfect for meal prep, and will keep you feeling full all morning long. This recipe also creates the perfect base for adding any of your favorite breakfast toppings!

1 Spray the inner pot with nonstick cooking spray.

2 Add the steel-cut oats, almond milk, brown sugar, and honey to the pot. Stir to combine.

3 Close and lock the lid, then turn the steam release handle to sealing. Select **Pressure Cook (high)** and set the cook time for **5 minutes**. When the cook time is complete, allow the pressure to release naturally for 10 minutes, then quick release the remaining pressure and remove the lid.

4 Divide ½-cup servings into 4 meal prep containers. Store in the fridge for up to 6 days or freeze for up to 2 months.

Reheating: Microwave each thawed serving for 1½ to 2 minutes. (If the oatmeal is dry after reheating, add a few teaspoons of milk or water and then stir.)

tip *If desired, top with ½ cup sliced banana, ½ cup sliced strawberries, ½ cup fresh blueberries, or 2 tablespoons peanut butter*

Nutrition per serving:
CALORIES: 195; **TOTAL FAT:** 4g; **SATURATED FAT:** 1g; **CHOLESTEROL:** 0mg; **SODIUM:** 123mg; **TOTAL CARBOHYDRATE:** 34g; **FIBER:** 5g; **PROTEIN:** 7g

MISSISSIPPI POT ROAST

Homemade ranch seasonings and no butter make this a healthier version of a traditional recipe! Removing the less-healthy ingredients allows the flavors of the parsley, dill, and pepperoncini to shine.

 SERVES: 8
SERVING SIZE: ¾ CUP ROAST

 PREP: 15 MINUTES
PRESSURE: 1 HOUR
TOTAL: 1 HOUR 25 MINUTES

 SETTINGS: PRESSURE COOK
RELEASE: NATURAL/QUICK

1 In a small bowl, combine the parsley, garlic powder, onion powder, and dill. Rub the spice mixture evenly over the chuck roast.

2 Select **Sauté** and add the olive oil to the bottom of the inner pot. When the oil begins to shimmer, place the roast in the pot and brown for 2–3 minutes on each side. Place the pepperoncini on top of the roast and add the pepperoncini juice, Worcestershire sauce, and beef broth.

3 Close and lock the lid, then turn the steam release handle to sealing. Select **Pressure Cook (high)** and set the cook time for **60 minutes**.

4 While the roast is cooking, divide the carrot and celery sticks equally between 8 meal prep containers.

5 When the cook time for the roast is complete, allow the pressure to naturally release for 10 minutes, then quick release the remaining pressure and remove the lid. Use two forks to shred the roast, then divide ¾-cup servings into the meal prep containers. Store in the fridge for up to 6 days or freeze for up to 2 months.

Reheating: Microwave each thawed serving for 1½ to 2 minutes.

1 tbsp dried parsley

1½ tsp garlic powder

1½ tsp onion powder

1 tsp dried dill weed

3lb (1.35kg) chuck roast

2 tbsp extra virgin olive oil

8 jarred pepperoncini peppers plus ¼ cup juice from the peppers

1 tsp Worcestershire sauce

1 cup low-sodium beef broth

1lb (455g) carrots, washed and cut into sticks

2 stalks celery, washed and cut into sticks

Nutrition per serving:
CALORIES: 367; **TOTAL FAT:** 23g; **SATURATED FAT:** 9g; **CHOLESTEROL:** 117mg; **SODIUM:** 249mg; **TOTAL CARBOHYDRATE:** 6g; **FIBER:** 2g; **PROTEIN:** 34g

SERVES: 8
SERVING SIZE: ¾ CUP

PREP: 15 MINUTES
PRESSURE: 6 MINUTES
TOTAL: 26 MINUTES

SETTINGS: SAUTÉ/PRESSURE COOK
RELEASE: QUICK

1 tbsp olive oil

1lb (450g) boneless, skinless chicken thighs, cut into cubes

1 shallot, minced

16oz (455g) baby bella mushrooms, sliced

1 cup quartered asparagus spears

3 cloves minced garlic

1½ cups uncooked Arborio rice

3 cups low-sodium vegetable broth

⅛ tsp salt

⅛ tsp black pepper

¼ cup shredded Parmesan cheese

CHICKEN AND VEGETABLE RISOTTO

This hearty meal is a healthy take on a traditional comfort food. Baby bella mushrooms and asparagus paired with garlic and shallots make this recipe feel indulgent, but it's easy to cook in the Instant Pot!

1 Select **Sauté** and add the olive oil to the pot.

2 When the oil begins to shimmer, add the chicken pieces, shallots, mushrooms, asparagus, and garlic. Sauté for 5 minutes or until the shallots are translucent and the chicken is lightly browned, then stir in the rice, vegetable broth, salt, and black pepper.

3 Close and lock the lid, then turn the steam release handle to sealing. Select **Pressure Cook (high)** and set the cook time for **6 minutes**. When the cook time is complete, quick release the pressure, remove the lid, and stir in the Parmesan cheese.

4 Divide ¾-cup servings into 8 meal prep containers. Store in the fridge for up to 6 days or freeze for up to 2 months.

Reheating: Microwave each thawed serving 1 to 1½ minutes, stirring halfway through reheating.

tip *To make this dish vegetarian, omit the chicken, skip the sautéing step, and just add all of the ingredients to the pot. The pressure cook time will remain the same.*

Nutrition per serving:
CALORIES: 253; **TOTAL FAT:** 5g; **SATURATED FAT:** 1g; **CHOLESTEROL:** 56mg; **SODIUM:** 105mg; **TOTAL CARBOHYDRATE:** 35g; **FIBER:** 2g; **PROTEIN:** 17g

LIGHTENED-UP CHEESECAKE
with Sliced Strawberries

This delectable cheesecake has the perfect balance of sweet and creamy flavors. Using cottage cheese and Greek yogurt helps make this recipe lighter, but you won't notice the difference!

SERVES: 8
SERVING SIZE: 1 SLICE

PREP: 15 MINUTES
PRESSURE: 35 MINUTES
TOTAL: 3 HOURS 10 MINUTES

SETTINGS: PRESSURE COOK
RELEASE: NATURAL

1 Add 2 cups of water to the inner pot and spray a 7-inch, oven-safe springform pan with nonstick cooking spray.

2 Begin making the crust by combining the oats, honey, and butter in a food processor. Process for 1–2 minutes or until the oats are chopped and a dough begins to form. Use the bottom of a drinking glass to firmly press the dough into the bottom of the prepared pan.

3 Begin making the filling by combining the cottage cheese, Greek yogurt, eggs, honey, whole wheat flour, and vanilla extract in a food processor. Process until smooth, pour the filling over the crust, then tightly cover the pan with aluminum foil. Place the cheesecake on the trivet and grasp the handles to carefully lower the pan into the pot.

4 Close and lock the lid, then turn the steam release handle to sealing. Select **Pressure Cook (high)** and set the cook time for **35 minutes**. When the cook time is complete, allow the pressure to release naturally—about 15 minutes—then remove the lid.

5 Use oven mitts to grasp the handles of the trivet and carefully remove the cheesecake from the pot. Remove the foil and immediately transfer the cheesecake to the refrigerator to cool and set for a minimum of 2 hours or until any extra moisture has evaporated.

6 Carefully remove the springform pan and cut the cheesecake into 8 equal slices. Place the slices in 8 meal prep containers and garnish with the sliced strawberries. Store in the fridge for up to 6 days. (This recipe cannot be frozen.)

FOR THE CRUST
⅔ cup rolled oats
1½ tbsp honey
1½ tbsp butter

FOR THE FILLING
2⅔ cups 2% cottage cheese
⅔ cup plain 2% Greek yogurt
3 eggs
4 tbsp honey
1½ tbsp whole wheat flour
1½ tsp vanilla extract
⅔ cup sliced fresh strawberries, for topping

tip *If preferred, you also can blend the strawberries into the filling by adding them to the food processor in step 3.*

Nutrition per serving:
CALORIES: 191; **TOTAL FAT:** 5g; **SATURATED FAT:** 3g; **CHOLESTEROL:** 71mg; **SODIUM:** 338mg; **TOTAL CARBOHYDRATE:** 21g; **FIBER:** 1g; **PROTEIN:** 14g

WEEK SEVEN
PREP PLAN

WEEK SEVEN PREP PLAN

Meals for this week include a filling Southwest Breakfast Casserole with black beans and potatoes, Lemon Chicken with Potatoes, Spicy Pork Carnitas, and my favorite comfort food with a healthier twist—Philly Cheesesteak Pasta. All of these recipes are made with minimally processed ingredients, so you can feel good about prepping them.

If desired, you can substitute one or more of the alternate recipes for the primary recipes in a plan. I often will make one of the alternate recipes during a prep day and freeze it in single-serving containers to thaw and reheat later. In order to integrate alternate recipes into your prep plan, reference the meal planning tips on pages 16 and 17 to determine how to swap alternate recipes into your prep session.

PREP PLAN YIELDS

SOUTHWEST BREAKFAST CASSEROLE

×6

LEMON CHICKEN WITH POTATOES

×6

RECORDS

PRIMARY

- Southwest Breakfast Casserole (p. 144)
- Lemon Chicken with Potatoes (p. 147)
- Philly Cheesesteak Pasta (p. 148)
- Spicy Pork Carnitas (p. 151)

ALTERNATE

- Blueberry Oatmeal Bake with Cream Cheese Filling (p. 152)
- Wild Rice and Mushroom Soup (p. 153)
- Easy Beef Stir-Fry (p. 154)
- Banana Oatmeal Bites (p. 155)

PHILLY CHEESESTEAK PASTA

×4

SPICY PORK CARNITAS

×8

SHOPPING LIST

PRODUCE

- [ ] 2 small red bell peppers
- [ ] 1 medium red bell pepper
- [ ] 2 small orange bell peppers
- [ ] 1 medium green bell pepper
- [ ] 1 medium red onion
- [ ] 1 small red onion
- [ ] 2 medium yellow onions
- [ ] 3 tbsp minced garlic
- [ ] 1 head cauliflower
- [ ] 3 lemons
- [ ] 1½lb (680g) mini potatoes, any variety
- [ ] 4 small russet potatoes
- [ ] 1 bunch fresh cilantro
- [ ] 1lb (455g) baby bella mushrooms
- [ ] 1lb (455g) asparagus

MEAT & DAIRY

- [ ] 2lb (900g) ground turkey
- [ ] 3lb (1.35kg) pork tenderloin
- [ ] 2lb (905g) lean ground beef
- [ ] 3lb (1.35kg) boneless, skinless chicken thighs
- [ ] 3 cups shredded cheddar cheese (1 cup optional for breakfast casserole)
- [ ] ⅓ cup plain 2% Greek yogurt
- [ ] 12 eggs

PANTRY & DRY GOODS

- [ ] 2 x 15oz (425) cans corn
- [ ] 2 x 15oz (425) cans black beans
- [ ] 2 x 4oz (115g) cans diced green chiles
- [ ] 14oz (395g) can diced tomatoes with green chiles
- [ ] 16 small whole wheat tortillas
- [ ] ¼ cup cornstarch
- [ ] 16oz (455g) box wheat elbow pasta
- [ ] ¼ cup low-sodium chicken broth
- [ ] Nonstick cooking spray

SPICES & SEASONINGS

- [ ] 4 tsp chili powder
- [ ] 2 tsp ground cumin
- [ ] 1 tsp ground coriander
- [ ] 1 tsp garlic salt
- [ ] 2½ tsp onion powder
- [ ] 1¼ tsp black pepper
- [ ] 2 tsp cayenne pepper (optional for carnitas)
- [ ] 2 bay leaves
- [ ] 1¼ tsp salt
- [ ] 2½ tsp paprika
- [ ] 2 tsp dried oregano
- [ ] 1 tsp marjoram

EQUIPMENT

- [ ] 6qt Instant Pot and trivet
- [ ] 24 meal prep containers
- [ ] 7in round baking pan or oven-safe dish
- [ ] 2 small bowls
- [ ] 2 medium bowls
- [ ] Chef's knife
- [ ] Slotted spoon
- [ ] Wooden spoon
- [ ] Cutting board
- [ ] Vegetable peeler
- [ ] Food processor or handheld shredder
- [ ] Aluminum foil
- [ ] Small resealable storage bacgs

PREP PLAN

(Total Estimated Time: 4½ to 5 hours)

1 Spray the inner pot with nonstick cooking spray and follow steps 1–4 to cook the pork tenderloin pieces for the **Spicy Pork Carnitas (p. 151)**.

2 While the tenderloin pieces are cooking, dice the bell peppers, onion, and cauliflower for the **Philly Cheesesteak Pasta (p. 148)**. Set the vegetables aside and combine the spices for the pasta in a small bowl.

3 Dice the bell peppers and onions, and shred the potatoes for the **Southwest Breakfast Casserole (p. 144)**. (You'll be making two batches of the casserole and cooking them separately in the pot, but they can be prepped at the same time.) Measure the spices and prepare the canned ingredients for the breakfast casserole. Set aside.

4 When the pork tenderloin pieces are finished cooking, quick release the pressure and remove the lid. Remove the bay leaves and continue with step 4 to shred the pork. Follow step 5 to brown the meat and then transfer 1-cup servings into 8 meal prep containers. Top each serving with chopped cilantro and place the tortillas in storage bags to complete the recipe.

5 Wash the inner pot and spray with nonstick cooking spray. Follow steps 1–4 to cook the Philly cheesesteak pasta.

6 When the cook time for the Philly cheesesteak pasta is complete, continue with step 5 to complete the recipe. Wash the inner pot, spray it with nonstick cooking spray, and place it back in the base.

7 Follow steps 1–3 to sauté the first batch of ground turkey for the breakfast casserole by placing half of the ground turkey, half of the prepared spices, and half of the prepared vegetables in the pot. When the first batch is complete, use a slotted spoon to transfer the cooked turkey to a plate to cool. Repeat steps 1–3 to sauté the second batch of ground turkey.

8 Spray a 7-inch oven-safe baking dish with nonstick cooking spray and transfer the first batch of cooked turkey to the prepared dish. Follow steps 4–8 to cook the first batch of the casserole.

9 While the casserole is cooking, prep the vegetables and spices for the **Lemon Chicken with Potatoes (p. 147)** and set aside.

10 After the cook time for the casserole is complete, remove it from the pot and set it aside to cool for 5–10 minutes. Repeat steps 4–8 to cook the second batch of the casserole, then follow step 9 to transfer the servings to meal prep containers and complete the recipe.

11 Wash the inner pot and place it back in the base. Spray the bottom of the pot with nonstick cooking spray and follow steps 1–3 to sear the chicken thighs for the lemon chicken with potatoes.

12 Follow steps 4–6 to complete the cooking of the lemon chicken with potatoes, then follow step 7 to transfer the servings to meal prep containers and complete the recipe.

SERVES: 6
SERVING SIZE: 1 CUP

PREP: 15 MINUTES
PRESSURE: 25 MINUTES
TOTAL: 40 MINUTES

SETTINGS: PRESSURE COOK
RELEASE: QUICK

1lb (450g) ground turkey

1 tsp chili powder

1 tsp ground cumin

½ tsp ground coriander

½ tsp garlic salt

½ tsp onion powder

⅛ tsp salt

⅛ tsp black pepper

1 small red bell pepper, seeded and diced

1 small orange bell pepper, seeded and diced

½ small red onion, diced

½ cup shredded cheddar cheese (optional)

2 small russet potatoes, shredded (about 3 cups)

15oz (425g) can of corn, drained

15oz (425g) can of black beans, drained

6 eggs

---

tip *To make this vegetarian, replace the turkey with one can of black beans and 8oz (225g) diced button mushrooms. Sauté the mushrooms with the peppers and onions, and add the beans in step 5. The cook time remains the same.*

SOUTHWEST BREAKFAST CASSEROLE

Hearty ground turkey, black beans, and vegetables make this spicy and flavorful casserole a favorite that you can eat for any meal! The high protein and slow-burning carbs will help keep you feeling full.

1 Spray the bottom of the inner pot with nonstick cooking spray. Select **Sauté.**

2 When the pot is hot, add the turkey, chili powder, cumin, coriander, garlic salt, onion powder, salt, and black pepper. Sauté for 2–3 minutes, then add the peppers and onions. Continue sautéing for 5–7 minutes or until the turkey is no longer pink.

3 Use a slotted spoon to transfer the turkey and vegetables to a medium bowl, then set aside. (If you are using the cheddar cheese, mix it in with the turkey and vegetables at this step).

4 Rinse the inner pot and place it back in the base. Add 1½ cups of water to the bottom of the pot and spray a 7-inch round baking pan or oven-safe dish with nonstick cooking spray.

5 Layer the ingredients into the pan, starting with the shredded potatoes, followed by the turkey and vegetable mixture, then the corn and black beans.

6 In a medium bowl, whisk the eggs, then pour them over the top of the casserole.

7 Cover the pan with foil, then place the pan on the trivet and grasp the handles to carefully lower it into the pot.

8 Close and lock the lid, then turn the steam release handle to sealing. Select **Pressure Cook (high)** and set the cook time for **25 minutes.** When the cook time is complete, quick release the pressure and remove the lid. Use oven mitts to grasp the trivet handles and carefully remove the pan from the pot, then remove the foil from the pan.

9 Divide 1-cup servings into 6 meal prep containers. Store in the fridge for up to 6 days or freeze for up to 2 months.

Reheating: Microwave each thawed serving for 1 to 1½ minutes.

Nutrition per serving:
CALORIES: 419; **TOTAL FAT:** 15g; **SATURATED FAT:** 5g; **CHOLESTEROL:** 230mg; **SODIUM:** 310mg; **TOTAL CARBOHYDRATE:** 42g; **FIBER:** 9g; **PROTEIN:** 32g

LEMON CHICKEN
with Potatoes

This light and filling dish features the tastes of lemon and garlic. Mini potatoes, baby Portobello mushrooms, and asparagus are also cooked right in the pot for easy cleanup.

1 Spray the bottom of the inner pot with nonstick cooking spray and select **Sauté**.

2 In a small bowl, combine the garlic, paprika, oregano, marjoram, salt, and black pepper. Rub the mixture into the tops of the chicken thighs.

3 Place a few of the chicken thighs seasoned sides down in the pot. Sear for 30 seconds to 1 minute per side, then transfer the thighs to a bowl. Repeat the process with the remaining thighs. When all of the thighs have been seared, add the lemon juice and chicken broth to the pot and use a wooden spoon to loosen any browned bits from the bottom of the pot.

4 Place the potatoes in the bottom of the pot, then place the chicken thighs on top of the potatoes. Close and lock the lid, then turn the steam release handle to sealing. Select **Pressure Cook (high)** and set the cook time for **5 minutes**. When the cook time is complete, quick release the pressure and remove the lid.

5 Add the mushrooms and asparagus on top of the chicken and close and lock the lid again. Turn the steam release handle to sealing, then select **Pressure Cook (high)** and set the cook time for **1 minute**.

6 When the cook time is complete, quick release the pressure and transfer the vegetables, chicken, and potatoes to a large platter. Select **Sauté** and add the cornstarch to the pot. Whisk the cornstarch into the broth until the gravy thickens, then remove the inner pot from the base.

7 Divide equal portions of the chicken, vegetables, and potatoes into 6 meal prep containers. Serve the gravy on the side or spoon it over the top of each serving prior to sealing the containers. Store in the fridge for up to 6 days or freeze for up to 2 months.

Reheating: Microwave each thawed serving for 1 to 1½ minutes.

SERVES: 6
SERVING SIZE: 2 CHICKEN THIGHS, 1 CUP VEGETABLES & 2 TO 4 POTATOES (DEPENDING ON SIZE)

PREP: 10 MINUTES
PRESSURE: 6 MINUTES
TOTAL: 21 MINUTES

SETTINGS: SAUTÉ/PRESSURE COOK
RELEASE: QUICK

2 tbsp minced garlic

1 tsp paprika

2 tsp dried oregano

1 tsp marjoram

½ tsp salt

½ tsp black pepper

3lb (1.35kg) boneless, skinless chicken thighs

Juice of 3 lemons

¼ cup chicken broth

1½lb (680g) mini potatoes (any variety)

1lb (455g) baby bella mushrooms, halved

1lb (455g) asparagus, halved and woody ends removed

2 tbsp cornstarch

Nutrition per serving:
CALORIES: 401; **TOTAL FAT:** 10g; **SATURATED FAT:** 2g; **CHOLESTEROL:** 215mg; **SODIUM:** 218mg; **TOTAL CARBOHYDRATE:** 29g; **FIBER:** 5g; **PROTEIN:** 50g;

SERVES: 4
SERVING SIZE: 1¼ CUPS

PREP: 15 MINUTES
PRESSURE: 2 MINUTES
TOTAL: 19 MINUTES

SETTINGS: PRESSURE COOK
RELEASE: QUICK

2lb (905g) lean ground beef

½ tsp salt

½ tsp black pepper

1½ tsp paprika

1½ tsp onion powder

2 tbsp cornstarch

16oz (455g) wheat elbow pasta

1 medium green bell pepper,
   seeded and diced

1 medium red bell pepper,
   seeded and diced

½ medium red onion, diced

1 tbsp minced garlic

2 cups finely diced cauliflower

2½ cups water

⅓ cup plain 2% Greek yogurt

2 cups shredded cheddar cheese

PHILLY CHEESESTEAK PASTA

Creamy, savory, and cheesy—this easy, skillet-like meal is packed with vegetables and flavor! Ground beef, pasta, peppers, and onions come together for a comforting meal that's made all in just one pot.

1 Spray the bottom of the pot with nonstick cooking spray and select **Sauté**.

2 When the pot is hot, add the ground beef, salt, black pepper, paprika, and onion powder. Sauté until the beef is no longer pink—about 10 minutes—then drain the ground beef and immediately add it back to the pot.

3 Add the cornstarch and stir, then pour the pasta on top of the beef and add green and red bell peppers, onions, garlic, cauliflower, and water.

4 Close and lock the lid, then turn the steam release handle to sealing. Select **Pressure Cook (high)** and set the cook time for **2 minutes**. When the cook time is complete, quick release the pressure and remove the lid. Drain any remaining liquid from the pot, then add the Greek yogurt and cheddar cheese, and stir until fully incorporated.

5 Divide 1¼-cup servings into 8 meal prep containers. Store in the fridge for up to 6 days or freeze for up to 2 months.

Reheating: Microwave each thawed portion for 45 seconds to 1 minute.

Nutrition per serving:
CALORIES: 1082; **TOTAL FAT:** 44g; **SATURATED FAT:** 22g; **CHOLESTEROL:** 208g; **SODIUM:** 535mg; **TOTAL CARBOHYDRATE:** 97g; **FIBER:** 2g; **PROTEIN:** 80g

SPICY PORK CARNITAS

I love this recipe because it's so flavorful and easy! This shredded pork tenderloin with green chiles, diced tomatoes, and chili pepper is the perfect tortilla filling.

1 Spray the inner pot with nonstick cooking spray.

2 Layer the onion slices into the bottom of the pot. (These will elevate the pork off the bottom of the pot and avoid a burn warning.) Add the green chiles on top of the onions, then place the pork tenderloin on top of the onions and chiles.

3 Sprinkle the chili powder and cayenne pepper (if using) over the top of the pork, then pour the diced tomatoes with green chiles on top of the pork, but do not stir. Add the bay leaves on top.

4 Close and lock the lid, then turn the steam release handle to sealing. Select **Pressure Cook (high)** and set the cook time for **45 minutes**. When the cook time is complete, quick release the pressure and remove the lid. Remove and discard the bay leaves, then transfer the pork to a large bowl and use two forks or a hand mixer to shred.

5 Carefully drain any remaining liquid from the pot and select **Sauté**. Add the olive oil and then add the shredded pork. Allow the meat to cook for 5 minutes, gently stirring, until the meat begins to brown.

6 Divide 1-cup servings into 8 meal prep containers, then top each serving with the chopped cilantro. Divide the tortillas into 8 resealable storage bags. When ready to serve, reheat the carnitas and place in the tortillas. Store in the fridge for up to 6 days or freeze for up to 2 months.

Reheating: Microwave each thawed serving for 1 to 1½ minutes.

SERVES: 8
SERVING SIZE: 1 CUP CARNITAS & 2 TORTILLAS

PREP: 10 MINUTES
PRESSURE: 45 MINUTES
TOTAL: 55 MINUTES

SETTINGS: PRESSURE COOK/SAUTÉ
RELEASE: QUICK

---

2 medium yellow onions, sliced thick

2 x 4oz (115g) cans diced green chilies

3lb (1.35kg) pork tenderloin

2 tsp chili powder

2 tsp cayenne pepper (optional)

14oz (395g) can diced tomatoes with green chiles

2 bay leaves

1 tbsp olive oil

½ cup chopped fresh cilantro

16 whole-wheat tortillas

---

tip *Other optional toppings (not included in nutrition information): shredded lettuce, chopped tomatoes, plain Greek yogurt, salsa, or shredded Monterey Jack cheese.*

Nutrition per serving:
CALORIES: 497; **TOTAL FAT:** 12g; **SATURATED FAT:** 4g; **CHOLESTEROL:** 111mg; **SODIUM:** 761mg; **TOTAL CARBOHYDRATE:** 51g; **FIBER:** 8g; **PROTEIN:** 44g

SERVES: 8
SERVING SIZE: 1 SLICE

PREP: 15 MINUTES
PRESSURE: 50 MINUTES
TOTAL: 1 HOUR 5 MINUTES

SETTINGS: PRESSURE COOK
RELEASE: QUICK

---

1 cup plain, unsweetened almond milk

½ cup wheat flour

3 eggs

2½ tsp baking powder

2 tsp vanilla extract

2 tsp ground cinnamon

½ tsp ground nutmeg

¼ tsp salt

3 cups rolled oats, divided

8oz (225g) cream cheese, warmed to room temperature

1 cup coconut sugar, divided

2 tbsp butter, softened

6oz (170g) fresh blueberries, rinsed and drained

BLUEBERRY OATMEAL BAKE *with Cream Cheese Filling*

This hearty and filling bake is made with sweet cream cheese and topped with an oat crumble topping. The oats in the recipe will keep you full, while the sweetened filling and topping will satisfy your sweet tooth!

1 Add 1 cup of water to the bottom of the pot. Spray a 7-inch round baking pan or oven-safe dish with nonstick cooking spray.

2 In a medium bowl, combine the almond milk, wheat flour, eggs, baking powder, vanilla extract, cinnamon, nutmeg, salt, and 2 cups of the oats. Mix well and then gently fold in the blueberries. Pour just enough of the mixture into the prepared baking pan so that the bottom of the pan is covered. Set the rest of the mixture aside.

3 Combine the cream cheese and ¾ cup of the coconut sugar in a medium bowl. Use a handheld mixer or food processor to combine, then spread the mixture over the top of the oatmeal mixture, keeping it about ½ inch away from the sides of the pan to allow the oatmeal to form a crust around the cream cheese layer. Pour the remaining oatmeal mixture on top of the cream cheese layer.

4 In a medium bowl, combine the remaining ¼ cup of the coconut sugar, the remaining cup of oats, and butter, and mash the ingredients together with a fork. Sprinkle the mixture over the top of the oatmeal bake, then cover the pan with foil. Place the pan on the trivet and grasp the handles to carefully lower the pan into the pot.

5 Close and lock the lid, then turn the steam release handle to sealing. Select **Pressure Cook (high)** and set the cook time for **50 minutes**. When the cook time is complete, quick release the pressure and remove the lid.

6 Allow the bake to cool for 30 minutes before cutting it into 8 equal-sized slices and placing them in meal prep containers. Store in the fridge for up to 6 days or freeze for up to 2 months.

Reheating: Microwave each thawed serving for 45 seconds to 1 minute. (If the bake seems dry, add a teaspoon or two of almond milk before reheating.)

Nutrition per serving:
CALORIES: 373; **TOTAL FAT:** 18g; **SATURATED FAT:** 8g; **CHOLESTEROL:** 100mg; **SODIUM:** 198mg; **TOTAL CARBOHYDRATE:** 49g; **FIBER:** 4g; **PROTEIN:** 9g

WILD RICE AND MUSHROOM SOUP

This light, but flavorful, soup is delicately seasoned with garlic, thyme, and oregano. Whole-grain wild rice, hearty mushrooms, and zucchini make this a filling meal!

SERVES: 6
SERVING SIZE: 1⅔ CUPS

PREP: 10 MINUTES
PRESSURE: 23 MINUTES
TOTAL: 43 MINUTES

SETTINGS: PRESSURE COOK
RELEASE: NATURAL

1 Spray the bottom of the inner pot with nonstick cooking spray and select **Sauté**.

2 Add the mushrooms, zucchini, celery, garlic, thyme, oregano, sage, marjoram, and salt to the pot. Sauté 2–3 minutes or just until the seasonings are fragrant, then add the wild rice, cannellini beans, and vegetable broth.

3 Close and lock the lid, then turn the steam release handle to sealing. Select **Pressure Cook (high)** and set the cook time for **23 minutes**. When the cook time is complete, allow the pressure to release naturally, then remove the lid.

4 Divide 1⅔-cup servings into 6 meal prep containers. Store in the fridge for up to 6 days or freeze for up to 2 months.

Reheating: Microwave each thawed serving for 1 to 1½ minutes.

1lb (450g) baby Portobello mushrooms, sliced

1 small zucchini, diced

2 stalks celery, diced

2 tbsp minced garlic

1 tbsp dried thyme

1 tbsp dried oregano

1 tsp sage

1 tsp marjoram

½ tsp salt

1 cup uncooked wild rice

14oz (395g) can cannellini beans, drained

64fl oz (415ml) low-sodium vegetable broth

Nutrition per serving:
CALORIES: 212; **TOTAL FAT:** 1g; **SATURATED FAT:** 1g; **CHOLESTEROL:** 0mg; **SODIUM:** 350mg; **TOTAL CARBOHYDRATE:** 43g; **FIBER:** 6g; **PROTEIN:** 11g

SERVES: 6
SERVING SIZE: ½ CUP RICE &
1¾ CUPS BEEF AND VEGETABLES

PREP: 10 MINUTES
PRESSURE: 25 MINUTES
TOTAL: 35 MINUTES

SETTINGS: PRESSURE COOK
RELEASE: QUICK

1½ cups uncooked brown rice

1½ cups water

½ cup coconut aminos or reduced-sodium soy sauce

4 tbsp peanut butter

2 tbsp honey

4 tsp rice vinegar

4 tsp sesame oil

3 tsp minced ginger root

2lb (905g) flank steak, sliced against the grain and into strips

14oz (395g) can of bean sprouts

1 large carrot, peeled and chopped

1 small Portobello mushroom, chopped

1 small zucchini, chopped

½ medium red onion, diced

6 cups broccoli florets (about 3 heads)

EASY BEEF STIR-FRY

This easy meal uses a simple sauce made from low-sodium coconut aminos, peanut butter, honey, and ginger. It's packed with vegetables and is both satisfying and filling!

1 Spray the inner pot with nonstick cooking spray. Add the rice and water and follow the instructions for cooking brown rice (p. 27).

2 While the rice is cooking, prepare the sauce by combining the coconut aminos, peanut butter, honey, rice vinegar, sesame oil, and ginger root in a small bowl. Use a fork to whisk.

3 When the rice is done cooking, divide ½-cup portions into 6 meal prep containers. Set aside.

4 Rinse the inner pot and spray with nonstick cooking spray. Add the sliced beef and sauce to the pot. Stir until the beef is thoroughly coated in the sauce.

5 Close and lock the lid, then turn the steam release handle to sealing. Select **Pressure Cook (high)** and set the cook time for **4 minutes.** When the cook time is complete, quick release the pressure and remove the lid. Add all of the vegetables to the pot and close and lock the lid again. Turn the steam release handle to sealing, select **Pressure Cook (high)**, and set the cook time for **1 minute**. When the cook time is complete, quick release the pressure and remove the lid.

6 Divide 1¾-cup servings into the meal prep containers with the rice. Store in the fridge for up to 6 days or freeze for up to 2 months.

Reheating: Microwave each thawed serving for 1 to 1½ minutes.

Nutrition per serving:
CALORIES: 550; **TOTAL FAT:** 15g; **SATURATED FAT:** 5g; **CHOLESTEROL:** 91mg; **SODIUM:** 629mg; **TOTAL CARBOHYDRATE:** 61g; **FIBER:** 7g; **PROTEIN:** 44g

BANANA OATMEAL BITES

These banana and oatmeal bites are a lighter snack that will satisfy any sweet tooth! Instead of using traditional ingredients like flour and sugar, these bites are made with bananas, oats, and cinnamon.

 SERVES: 14
SERVING SIZE: 1 BITE

 PREP: 5 MINUTES
PRESSURE: 8 MINUTES
TOTAL: 23 MINUTES

 SETTINGS: PRESSURE COOK
RELEASE: QUICK

1 Place the trivet into the pot and add 1 cup of water. Spray 2 egg bite molds with nonstick cooking spray and set them aside.

2 Combine the bananas, oats, cinnamon, vanilla extract, and salt in a large bowl. Use a fork to mash the ingredients together, then fold in the chocolate chips (if using).

3 Fill each of the cups in the egg bite molds with the banana-oat mixture and then cover the molds with foil. Place both egg bite molds in the pot, ensuring the cups aren't stacked directly on top of one another.

4 Close and lock the lid, then turn the steam release handle to sealing. Select **Pressure Cook (high)** and set the cook time for **8 minutes**. When the cook time is complete, quick release the pressure and remove the lid. Use oven mitts to grasp the trivet handles and carefully remove the molds from the pot. Remove the foil and set the bites aside to cool for 10 minutes.

5 Once the bites have cooled, place a plate upside down on top of each mold and carefully flip the plate and mold to remove the bites from the molds. (If they don't come out easily, tap or gently squeeze the bottom of each cup to help them release.)

6 Place the bites in a large plastic bag or airtight plastic container and refrigerate until ready to eat. (These are best enjoyed chilled.) Store in the fridge for up to 6 days or freeze for up to 2 months.

4 ripe bananas, peeled

2 cups rolled oats

1⅓ tbsp ground cinnamon

2 tsp vanilla extract

¼ tsp salt

½ cup dark chocolate chips (optional)

tip *If desired, you can omit the chocolate chips or replace them with raisins.*

Nutrition per serving (including chocolate chips):
CALORIES: 109; **TOTAL FAT:** 3g; **SATURATED FAT:** 2g; **CHOLESTEROL:** 1mg; **SODIUM:** 49mg; **TOTAL CARBOHYDRATE:** 19g; **FIBER:** 2g; **PROTEIN:** 2g

INDEX

A

almond milk 25
Apple Cinnamon Baked Oatmeal 36–37
Apple Oat Crumble 119
Asian Chicken "Stir-Fry" with Ramen 74–75
asparagus (staple recipe) 28

B

Banana Bread with Peanut Butter Frosting 83
Banana Oatmeal Bites 155
basmati rice (staple recipe) 27
beef
 Beef Fajita Bowls 38–39
 Beef Gyros with Tzatziki Sauce 130–31
 Carne Asada Street Taco Bowls 58–59
 Easy Beef Stir-Fry 154
 Mississippi Pot Roast 135
 Philly Cheesesteak Pasta 148–49
Beef Fajita Bowls 38–39
Beef Gyros with Tzatziki Sauce 130–31
black rice (staple recipe) 27
Blueberry Oatmeal Bake with Cream Cheese Filling 152
bowls
 Beef Fajita Bowls 38–39
 Carne Asada Street Taco Bowls 58–59
 Chicken Burrito Bowls 45
 Honey Garlic Chicken Bowls 76–77
 Southwest Egg Roll in a Bowl 117
 Teriyaki Meatball Bowls 60–61
breads, Banana Bread with Peanut Butter Frosting 83
Breakfast Fried Rice 116
Breakfast Ratatouille 90–91
breakfasts
 Breakfast Fried Rice 116
 Breakfast Ratatouille 90–91
 Breakfast Sweet Potatoes 108–09
 Fajita Breakfast Casserole 44
 French Toast Casserole 126–27

 Light & Fluffy Egg Casserole 54–55
 Mini Egg Scrambles 62
 Southwest Breakfast Casserole 144–45
 Vegetable Frittata 72–73
Breakfast Sweet Potatoes 108–09
broccoli (staple recipe) 28
brown rice 24, 27
burn prevention 21
burritos
 Chicken Burrito Bowls 45
 Turkey Chorizo and Egg Breakfast Burritos 98

C

Carne Asada Street Taco Bowls 58–59
casseroles
 Cheesy Ranch Chicken Casserole 80
 Fajita Breakfast Casserole 44
 French Toast Casserole 126–27
 Light & Fluffy Egg Casserole 54–55
 Southwest Breakfast Casserole 144–45
 Spicy Enchilada Casserole 63
cauliflower (staple recipe) 29
Cheesy Ranch Chicken Casserole 80
chicken
 Asian Chicken "Stir-Fry" with Ramen 74–75
 Cheesy Ranch Chicken Casserole 80
 Chicken Lettuce Wraps 118
 Chicken Burrito Bowls 45
 Chicken and Rice with Broccoli and Mushrooms 92–93
 Chicken and Vegetable Risotto 136
 Honey Garlic Chicken Bowls 76–77
 Kung Pao Chicken 110–11
 Lemon Chicken with Potatoes 146–47
 Orange Chicken 64
 Spicy White Chicken Chili 112–13
 Tuscan Chicken Pasta 100
Chicken Lettuce Wraps 118
Chicken Lime Burrito Bowls 45
Chicken and Rice with Broccoli and Mushrooms 92–93
Chicken and Vegetable Risotto 136
chili
 Spicy White Chicken Chili 112–13
 Vegetarian Chili 96–97

R

S